THE END OF CHIVALRY

Library Edition published 1989
Published by Marshall Cavendish Corporation
147 West Merrick Road
Freeport, Long Island
N.Y. 11520

Typeset by Jamesway Graphics
Hanson Close Middleton Manchester M24 2HD
Printed in the USA by Worzalla Publishing
Company, Wisconsin

LIBRARY OF CONGRESS
Library of Congress Cataloging-in-Publication
Data

The End of Chivalry
   p. cm. – (Exploring the past: 3)
   Bibliography: p.
   Includes index.
   Summary: Describes the lives and times of
Henry V, Joan of Arc, and Richard III.
   ISBN 0–86307–996–2: $19.95.
   ISBN 0–86307–993–8 (set): $119.95
   1. Great Britain – History – Lancaster and
York, 1399–1485 – Biography – Juvenile
literature. 2. Great Britain – Kings and rulers –
Biography – Juvenile literature. 3. Henry V,
King of England, 1387–1422 – Juvenile
literature. 4. Richard III, King of England,
1452–1485 – Juvenile literature. 5. Joan of Arc,
Saint, 1412–1431 – Juvenile literature.
6. Christian saints – France – Biography –
Juvenile literature. 7. Chivalry – Juvenile
literature. [1. Great Britain – History –
Lancaster and York, 1399–1485. 2. Henry V.
King of England, 1387–1422. 3. Richard III,
King of England, 1452–1485. 4. Joan, of Arc,
Saint, 1412–1431. 5. Kings, queens, rulers, etc.
6. Saints.] I. Marshall Cavendish Corporation.
II. Series.
DA 245.E47 1989
942.04 – dc19   88-21643
                                     CIP
                                     AC

ISBN 0–86307–993–8 (set)
ISBN 0–86307–996–2 (vol)
The End of Chivalry is number three in the
Exploring the Past series.

Credits: Front cover: Nick Harris;
page 1: Peter Dennis; page 3: Bridgeman Art
Library

THE END OF
CHIVALRY

Henry V

Joan of Arc

Richard III

Marshall Cavendish

NEW YORK · TORONTO · LONDON · SYDNEY

STAFF LIST

Series Editor
Sue Lyon

Assistant Editors
Laura Buller
Jill Wiley

Art Editor
Keith Vollans

Production Controller
Tom Helsby

Managing Editor
Alan Ross

Editorial Consultant
Maggi McCormick

Publishing Manager
Robert Paulley

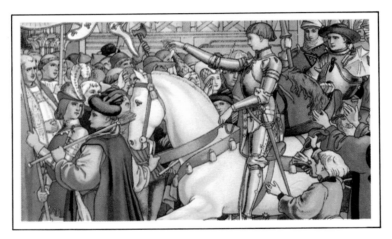

Titles in the EXPLORING THE PAST series

READER'S GUIDE

Imagine that you owned a time machine, and that you traveled back to the days when your parents were in school. Your hometown and school would look different, while the clothes, music, and magazines that your parents were enjoying might seem odd, perhaps amusing, and certainly "old fashioned" and "out of date." Travel back a few hundred years, and you would be astonished and fascinated by the strange food, homes, even language, of our ancestors.

Time machines do not yet exist, but in this book you can explore one of the most important periods of the past through the eyes of three people who made history happen. An introduction sets the scene and highlights the significant themes of the age, while the chronology lists important events and when they happened to help you to understand the background to the period. There is also a glossary to explain words that you may not understand and a list of other books that you may find useful.

The past is important to us all, for the world we know was formed by the actions of people who inhabited it before us. So, by understanding history, we can better understand the events of our own times. Perhaps that is why you will find exploring the past so exciting, rewarding and fascinating.

Peter Dennis

CONTENTS

Yale University/The Edwin Austen Abbey Memorial Collection

Bridgeman Art Library

INTRODUCTION

Talk of chivalry conjures up pictures of splendidly armored knights with elaborate codes of honor, dramatic tournaments where knights competed for their lady loves' favors, or knightly quests, pilgrimages and crusades—a romantic and improbable society with no more connection with real life than a fairy tale. But the cult of chivalry had a highly practical purpose in the Middle Ages.

The Development of Chivalry

Around the year A.D. 1000, the nobility was very far from chivalric. Brutish, scarcely Christianized, anarchic warriors, they rampaged across Europe, sacking towns and monasteries, looting and burning without restraint. In response, the Church (at that time, all of Europe was Roman Catholic) tried to control this violence by channeling the knights' fighting energies into Christian causes, such as the Crusades or other holy wars. The concept of the "Truce of God"—days when no fighting was permitted—was introduced, and the number of such days of peace increased. At the same time, the warring nobles themselves developed a code that forbade them to attack those weaker than themselves. Instead, they were to protect the powerless, who included peasants, clergy, and church property, and—last, but certainly not least, as shown by the love songs of the troubadours—women, who were elevated to an ideal status and whose favors were only to be won by arduous "ordeals." So, the concept of chivalry developed in medieval Europe, and with it came the ideal of the perfect knight, who was "without fear or reproach."

The Chivalrous Knight

The word "chivalry" is derived from chevalerie, an old French word meaning horse soldiers or cavalry, and the knight was first and foremost a man who fought on horseback. From the early Middle Ages, the mounted knight dominated the battlefield. The infantry (foot soldiers), made up of lightly armored and ill-trained peasants, was of little account and was easily scattered by the charges of the heavy horsemen. Trained from childhood, successively as a page and a squire in the arts of fighting, and finally "dubbed" a knight in a ceremony that was as much religious as military, the knight was the only reasonably professional soldier of his time. But, to the chivalrous knight, fighting was as much a sport as a job.

In peacetime, the high points of a knight's life were the tournaments, which, like modern football games, were great public spectacles. Tournaments had begun in the 11th century, mainly as melées, in which two opposed groups of knights fought each other—often with literally murderous results. Condemned by the Church as immoral and banned by the kings, who feared that the violence would spread beyond the melée, the tournament evolved into the joust. This was an individual combat between two knights that tested their skills at unhorsing one another, but which was not supposed to cause serious injury.

Resplendent in his armor and carrying the "favor"—a scarf or handkerchief—of his lady, the knight shone in all his military glory at the tournament. At the height of his power, the chivalrous knight was a combination of a high sense of honor, a "sporting" attitude to fighting, and a narrow class feeling that despised all those who were not nobly born. He appeared unchallenged and unchallengeable both morally—the knight firmly believed that God was on his side—and militarily.

The Changing Face of War

However, by the mid-14th century, the knights were no longer invincible on the battlefield. Although armor had grown heavier to deal with the threat posed by the crossbow—a deadly weapon, but so slow to fire that it was of more use in sieges than battles—important changes were taking place in methods of fighting.

In 1346, the flower of French chivalry, reputedly the finest in Christendom, rode in its splendor into battle at Crécy. The knights were playing the old chivalrous game, but the smaller English force under King Edward III that waited for them was dismounted. Behind sharp stakes driven into the ground, longbowmen rained down arrows that turned the charging cavalry into a chaotic rout. The longbow, which could be fired much faster than the crossbow and so could be used on the battlefield, was one of the signs of the coming end of chivalry.

The French nobles were slow to realize this, however. Ten years later at the battle of Poitiers, and even more disastrously at Agincourt in 1415, they rushed to their deaths bravely and blindly. The "unchivalrous" English, their tactics making up for their much smaller army, won.

Another deathblow to chivalry was gunpowder, first used in the Hundred Years' War (1337-1453). Even the most primitive cannons could slowly batter down the great castles behind whose mighty walls the nobility had lived out their lives, safe from outside interference. Now, when the royal

Mansell Collection; Edimage; John Bethell

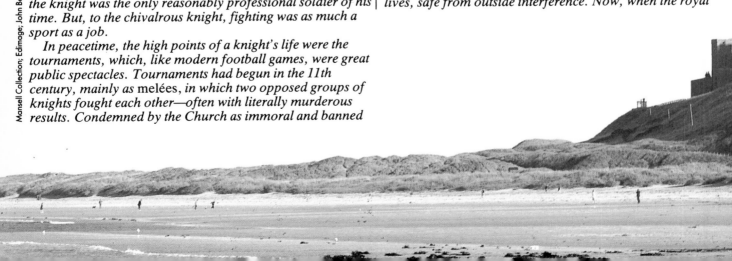

army arrived with its great cannons, the counts or knights looking down from the battlements knew that even the mightiest castle walls would crumble beneath the professional attentions of the guns.

The Break-up of Feudalism

Of course, professional gunners cost money—and money was another factor that undermined chivalry. The economic and social structure underpinning chivalry had originally been feudal—non-monetary, hierarchical, and immobile. Peasants plowed, and by their labors, supported priests, who prayed and had their own extensive hierarchy, and knights, who protected both priest and peasant from invasions or other disturbances. Knights also owed 40 days military service a year to their overlord, the king, duke, or count—the person at the top of the particular feudal "pyramid" or hierarchy.

The feudal system had seldom worked perfectly. Knights or barons quarreled with each other, they oppressed the peasantry, and from the early Middle Ages, mercenaries had been used to support the armored knights. But by the end of the 14th century, mercenaries were more important than his knights to a feudal overlord. The need for money began to govern policy: King Edward IV of England called off a war with France in 1475 in return for a huge cash payment.

With the break-up of feudalism, warfare itself grew increasingly ruthless and unchivalrous. (In fact, for the unarmored infantrymen, war had always been savage; ransoming captured knights was an important way of raising money in the Middle Ages, but no one bothered to ransom foot soldiers.) In the early Middle Ages, a knight or count had almost never attacked his feudal overlord, but now, in both France and England, crowns wobbled on the heads of weak kings, who were faced by overmighty subjects. In England, during the civil strife called the Wars of the Roses (1455-1487), Richard Neville, the Earl of Warwick was so powerful that he earned the title of "Kingmaker." He

deposed Henry VI, replaced him with Edward IV, and then, when he quarreled with Edward, restored Henry. In France, the great Dukes of Burgundy were often far stronger—because they were richer—than the French kings, their relatives and their supposed overlords. This Burgundian wealth came not from land, but from control of the rich trading towns of Flanders. Now, merchants' money counted for more than knightly prowess.

At the other end of the social scale, peasants suffered far more. Instead of limited wars, with the armies disbanding soon after, mercenary bands plundered the countryside as a way of life in the pauses between the everlasting wars. The Church, which had once controlled and lessened the effects of war, lacked its former prestige and authority. It had become too rich—it owned perhaps one-third of all the wealth in Europe—and too detached from people's religious needs. This produced an outburst of heresies, not all of which were easily crushed. When the Hussites of Bohemia (now Czechoslovakia) rebelled against the Church in 1419, the Pope called on Emperor Sigismund to lead a great army of knights against the rebels. But the Czechs, improvizing with fortified wagons (the first tanks), broke the Imperial cavalry in two great victories. This was unheard of—peasants and townsfolk triumphing over great nobles.

The Last Years of Chivalry
Paradoxically, in its twilight years, the cult of chivalry became even more elaborate and courtly. The Dukes of Burgundy may have owed their wealth to Flemish merchants' sober labor, but they spent it on a court whose aristocratic elegance outshone the rest of Europe and which has colored our own image of chivalry. Duke Philip the Good founded the Order of the Golden Fleece—a very exclusive chivalrous order—while in England, Edward III founded the Order of the Garter. Court dress became ever more fantastic: sleeves were so long that they fell to the ground, shoes were so pointed that they curled up and over almost to reach the knee. Banquets grew more and more exotic and expensive, with pies so huge that entire orchestras sat inside them to play. And the unreal romance of courtly love, first invented by the troubadours, became yet more elaborate and the noble ladies more idealized.

The romantic ideal of chivalry persisted and was cultivated long after it had lost its real purpose. In the 16th century, Henry VIII of England organized great chivalrous junkets, and Henry II of France was killed in a joust in 1559, true to French traditions of reckless bravery. In England, Elizabeth I encouraged the cult of her idealized self, and even in the 17th century Charles I used compulsory knighthoods (for which the knights had to pay) as a way to raise money. But Charles' half-chivalrous court was destroyed in the English Civil War and after that, chivalry was truly dead—at least as a social system. As an attitude of mind it perhaps still survives in the idea of a "gentleman" who cares for those weaker than himself.

Topham Picture Library

Geoffrey Wheeler

Henry V

E ven Henry V's French enemies saw him as a truly chivalrous knight: noble, brave, courteous, and religious. But Henry was no empty-headed, ill-disciplined horseman. Before pressing his claim to the French throne, Henry prepared carefully, gaining the support both of his subjects and of other rulers. And he used humble bowmen to destroy the brave, but reckless, charges of the French knights. His great victories in France restored English power, but Henry's achievements did not last. After his early death, the French, inspired by Joan of Arc, began to fight back, and under the rule of his weak son, England was plunged into civil war.

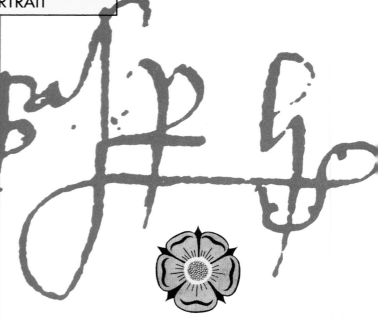

Nik Spender

Personal Profile

HENRY V
Born *September 16, 1387, Monmouth, Wales.*
Died *August 31, 1422, Vincennes, near Paris.*
Reign *1413–1422.*
Parents *Henry Bolingbroke (Henry IV), and Lady Mary de Bohun.*
Personal appearance *Slender, above average height, with brown hair, hazel eyes, a long straight nose and strong chin.*
General *A self-contained, pious man who loved books and music as well as hunting. Brave, generous, courteous and just, he inspired great loyalty.*

'King Henry the Fifth, too famous to live long'

These words of Shakespeare convey the grief of John, Duke of Bedford, as he mourned the death of his 34-year-old brother, Henry V. Indeed, all England grieved, for in the nine years that Henry reigned, he proved himself a worthy king, loved by his subjects at home and respected by his enemies abroad.

Yet at Henry's birth, on September 16, 1387, there was little to suggest the glorious future which awaited him. He was born plain Henry of Monmouth, during the troubled reign of Richard II. His mother was only 17 when Henry was born; and three sons and two daughters later, she died at the age of just 24. His father was Henry Bolingbroke, the King's cousin and one of his most powerful subjects.

Both Henry's father and his grandfather, John of Gaunt, were valiant knights who traveled widely at home and abroad. Henry and his brothers grew up listening to exciting tales of the long war with the French (later to be called the Hundred Years' War) and their father's crusades to Jerusalem. So, from an early age, Henry burned to have a glorious career worthy of his heritage.

As a great nobleman's eldest son, Henry was brought up to be a chivalrous knight. His education was brief and fragmented, but at nine he already owned a sword, a harp and seven books of grammar. He loved music and outdoor sports like riding, hunting, fishing and falconry,

THE CHASE
Young Henry was an athletic boy who loved fishing, falconry, riding and hunting—all normal pursuits for a young nobleman. It is said that he ran so fast, that with one or two friends, he could run down a deer.

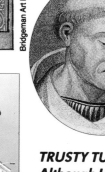

TRUSTY TUTOR
Although Henry had no formal schooling as we know it today, he was taught for a while by his uncle Henry Beaufort (above), a brilliant scholar. Beaufort remained Henry's most trusted advisor.

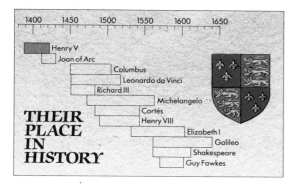

1400	1450	1500	1550	1600	1650

Henry V
Joan of Arc
Columbus
Leonardo da Vinci
Richard III
Michelangelo
Cortés
Henry VIII
Elizabeth I
Galileo
Shakespeare
Guy Fawkes

THEIR PLACE IN HISTORY

A CHANGE OF DESTINY
Henry was born in Monmouth, Wales (right). He later became Prince of Wales when his father seized the English crown.

and was tutored for a time by his brilliant uncle Henry Beaufort, Chancellor of Oxford University.

But Henry's boyhood ended abruptly soon after his 11th birthday. As a result of intrigues at court, his father was banished by Richard II, and Henry was taken into the Royal Court as a hostage. Yet he was well treated by the king, who seemed genuinely fond of him. He accompanied Richard on his successful campaign in Ireland, where Henry's bravery won him a knighthood on the field of battle. Then, just months later, his father returned from exile in France and seized the throne,

changing Henry's destiny.

Soon after his father's coronation in October, 1399, Henry was proclaimed Prince of Wales and heir to the throne, just as the Prince of Wales is today. But Henry had to earn his title the hard way—by fighting a long war against the Welsh who, led by Owen Glendower from his base in the mountains, had rebelled against their English overlords.

The experience Henry gained in Wales was invaluable. There, he learned to fight with few troops and little money, in bad weather and mountainous terrain,

Mansell Collection

BBC Hulton

Mansell Collection

A NEW KING
Henry was crowned at Westminster Abbey on March 21, 1413. His seals show him on the throne (far left) and in armor (above).

repulsing small bands of men and besieging castles. In 1403, he pawned his own jewels to pay his soldiers, realizing that regular payments would help win their loyalty.

The Prince proved himself an able commander and, from 1406 on, he played an increasingly important role in the King's Council. When his father became ill in 1410, Henry largely took over the job of government. But legend has it that off-duty, Henry was everything but serious and sober, and he behaved as "a rollicker" who would

Henry's French Connection

Philip IV of France

Louis X   Philip V   Charles IV   Isabella = Edward II of England

Edward III of England

Edward (the "Black Prince")   Lionel   John (of Gaunt)   Edmund   Thomas

Richard II

Henry IV

Henry V

A DUBIOUS CLAIM
(left) Henry firmly believed in his right to the French throne. His great-great-grandmother, Isabella, was the daughter of Philip IV of France, and when her brothers died without male heirs, the French crown was passed to another branch of the family.

HENRY'S BADGE

The Battle of Shrewsbury

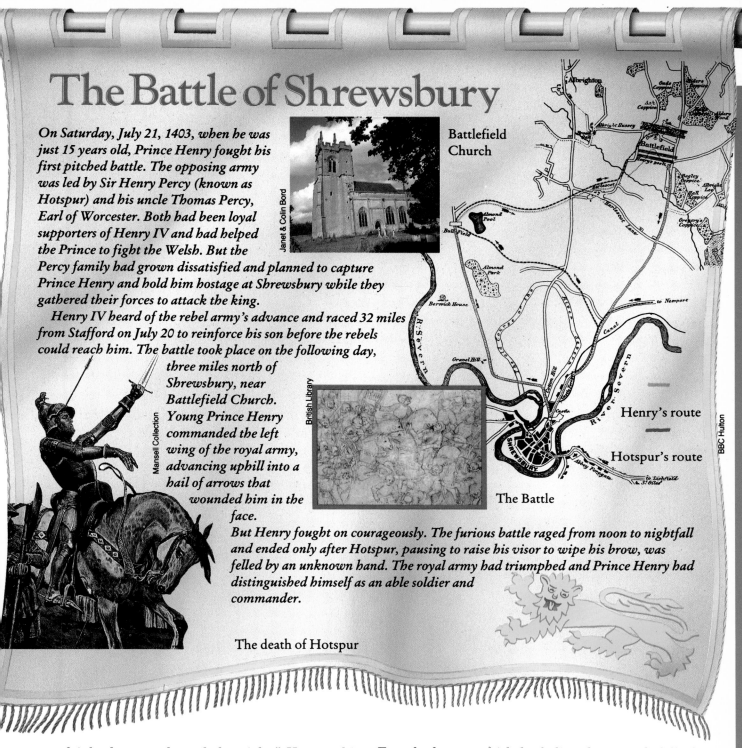

On Saturday, July 21, 1403, when he was just 15 years old, Prince Henry fought his first pitched battle. The opposing army was led by Sir Henry Percy (known as Hotspur) and his uncle Thomas Percy, Earl of Worcester. Both had been loyal supporters of Henry IV and had helped the Prince to fight the Welsh. But the Percy family had grown dissatisfied and planned to capture Prince Henry and hold him hostage at Shrewsbury while they gathered their forces to attack the king.

Henry IV heard of the rebel army's advance and raced 32 miles from Stafford on July 20 to reinforce his son before the rebels could reach him. The battle took place on the following day, three miles north of Shrewsbury, near Battlefield Church. Young Prince Henry commanded the left wing of the royal army, advancing uphill into a hail of arrows that wounded him in the face.

But Henry fought on courageously. The furious battle raged from noon to nightfall and ended only after Hotspur, pausing to raise his visor to wipe his brow, was felled by an unknown hand. The royal army had triumphed and Prince Henry had distinguished himself as an able soldier and commander.

Battlefield Church

Janet & Colin Bord

British Library

The Battle

Mansell Collection

Henry's route

Hotspur's route

BBC Hulton

The death of Hotspur

swear, drink, dance and revel the night." He put this youthful exuberance behind him, though, when his father died and he became king in 1413. In the words of the chronicler Thomas Walsingham, "as soon as he was made king he was changed suddenly into another man, zealous for honesty, modesty and gravity."

Henry was 25 when he was crowned; and, almost immediately, he focused his attention on France. He wanted to regain the lands there that had once belonged to the English and also to renew the English claim to the French throne, which he believed was rightfully his.

Preparations for war took two years. Huge sums of money were raised through taxes, loans and donations from people like Dick Whittington, London's Lord Mayor. Henry even pawned his crown jewels.

Henry successfully invaded France and besieged many French towns through four successive winters. He was ruthless in his desire to win. "War without fire," he said, "is no more worth than sausage without mustard." He led his army by example, demonstrating sound

Jarrold & Sons

military judgment and considerable bravery in battle. He was a strict leader, and some people have suggested that, far from being the ideal knight and warrior king, he was cruel and ruthless. In fact, Henry was probably compassionate for the time he lived in, and he was very religious, attributing his victories to God.

Five years of warfare and skillful diplomacy finally gave Henry what he wanted. In May, 1420, the French signed the Treaty of Troyes, recognizing Henry as Heir and Regent of France as soon as mad old Charles VI of France died. In the meantime, Henry married the king's attractive 19-year-old daughter, Catherine, and they had a son, Henry, who was later to become Henry VI—the only king to rule both England and France.

In following years, Henry continued to fight the Dauphin (the dispossessed heir to the French throne) and his supporters. But Henry grew ill, probably with dysentery, and finally died in France. Henry's body was brought to England and buried in Westminster Abbey.

Spectrum

MEMORIAL
Henry was buried in grand style at Westminster Abbey on November 7, 1422. His tomb lies in his own chapel (far left) and bears his effigy (left).

Personal Effects

Henry's few surviving possessions are mostly military in character, as befits a warrior king. The tournament helmet, shield and saddle (far right) were all carried in Henry's funeral procession. His shield was made from oak, and would have had the arms of England painted on a leather covering on the front. Today, only the faint remnant of an embroidered pattern on the inside is visible. The wooden saddle had a canvas seat stuffed with hay. The sword may not have been Henry's own, but he would certainly have had one like it.

This wooden cradle (below) is also said to be Henry's and would have traveled with the family from castle to castle.

Museum of London

Dean & Chapter of Westminster

AGINCOURT

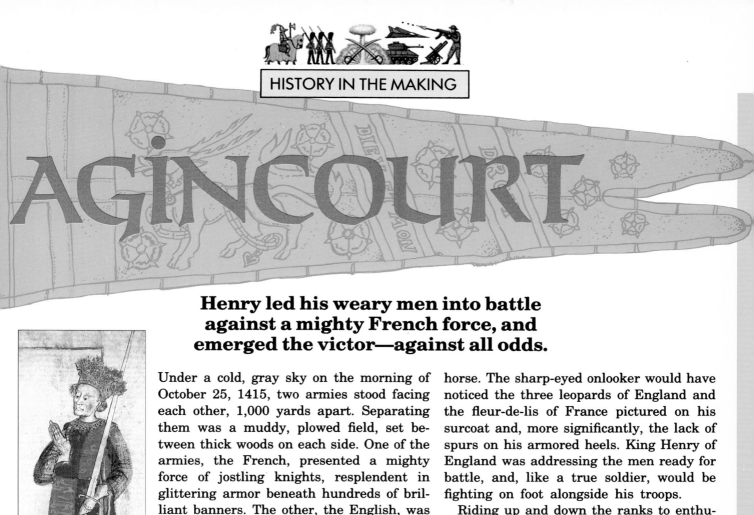

Henry led his weary men into battle against a mighty French force, and emerged the victor—against all odds.

Under a cold, gray sky on the morning of October 25, 1415, two armies stood facing each other, 1,000 yards apart. Separating them was a muddy, plowed field, set between thick woods on each side. One of the armies, the French, presented a mighty force of jostling knights, resplendent in glittering armor beneath hundreds of brilliant banners. The other, the English, was just a quarter the size—a small, compact band arranged in tight formation. Along its front rode a bare-headed knight on a small

GLORY FOR ENGLAND
When Henry V (left) went to war with the mad French King Charles VI (below right), he could not have dreamed of a victory more glorious than Agincourt (below).

British Library

Kobal Collection

horse. The sharp-eyed onlooker would have noticed the three leopards of England and the fleur-de-lis of France pictured on his surcoat and, more significantly, the lack of spurs on his armored heels. King Henry of England was addressing the men ready for battle, and, like a true soldier, would be fighting on foot alongside his troops.

Riding up and down the ranks to enthusiastic cheers, Henry encouraged his men with stirring words. And the soldiers certainly needed encouragement, for they had marched 260 miles in 17 days with barely enough rations for half that time. Most of them had to live on nuts and berries picked along the way, and many were suffering from diarrhea. Now, close to the tiny village of Agincourt, their road to Calais—and the

Mansell Collection

way home to England—was barred by the largest French army they had ever seen.

Ten weeks earlier, in mid-August, the English had landed, 10,000 strong, on the French coast and captured the port of Harfleur. But the capture had taken far longer than expected; and, by the time the town surrendered, one Englishman in five was dead, wounded, or too sick to fight. Henry also had to leave 1,200 men there to guard the town, and this left him with less than 6,000 soldiers with which to conquer France.

BANNERS ADVANCE!

At this point, most commanders would have cut their losses and sailed home. But not Henry. He knew that Harfleur was too small a prize for so much effort and expense, so he had to go on. Yet, now his army was too weak to march on to capture Paris as he had hoped to do. Eventually, he decided to march 160 miles across Northern France to Calais, an English-held port, to demonstrate that he was master of Normandy. If the French army could be tempted to fight him along the way, so much the better. As it turned out, the French army did challenge him, determined to smash the invaders.

For three hours they watched each other, but nothing happened. Henry knew his army's morale was as high as he could make it. The 900 men-at-arms and 5,000 bowmen were good soldiers. But they were exhausted and could not hold out without supplies much longer.

THE FRENCH CAVALRY COLLAPSES UNDER THE VICIOUS ARROW STORM

Tony Smith

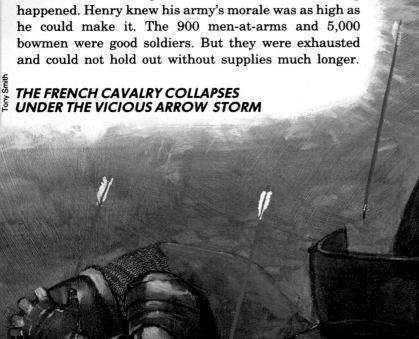

THE ROAD TO AGINCOURT

October 7th
Henry leaves Harfleur for Calais.

October 13th
Henry learns that the ford at the mouth of the Somme is guarded by 6,000 French and turns inland to look for another bridging point.

October 19th
The English army finally crosses the Somme near Nesle, 80 miles inland, having outmaneuvred the French.

October 20th
Henry is visited by French heralds who announce the French intention to fight. The English continue north toward Calais.

October 24th
English scouts report a massive French army assembling for battle. Henry makes a camp at Maisoncelles.

Finally, at around 11 a.m., Henry made his move. "Banners advance! In the name of Jesus, Mary and St. George," he cried. Trumpets blaring, the English trudged forward 700 yards. Within "extreme bowshot" (250–300 yards) of the enemy, the army halted and the archers hammered long, sharpened stakes into the ground, pointing toward the enemy. Henry was hoping to provoke the French into attacking him here, where they would have to squeeze between the woods on each side and have to charge over wet, sticky ground.

The French, however, were in confusion as the knights were eager to be first to attack. The commander,

Constable d'Albret, finally got the army into three lines, two on foot (each line perhaps eight deep and 8,000 strong) and the rear one mounted. Even so, 3,000 crossbowmen were sandwiched between the first two lines, with their firing line cut out by the unruly knights.

Suddenly, the English acted and the "air was darkened by an intolerable number of piercing arrows flying across the sky to pour upon the enemy like a cloud laden with rain." The arrow strike stung the French into life. Over 1,000 mounted knights lumbered forward to charge the English archers on the flanks. But, arrow after arrow found its target and only about 150 reached the stakes, where they were impaled or thrown from the saddle and hacked to death by the archers. The surviving horses fled in panic, charging straight into the first line of men-at-arms advancing on foot.

Though crippled by the arrow storm, the immense French first line staggered on toward Henry's royal banner in the center. This massive onslaught sent the English men-at-arms reeling "a spear's length." But the French were so packed together that they could not even use their weapons. Seeing the French disorder, the

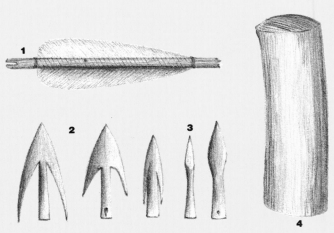

THE LONGBOW

The most feared weapon in the English army, the longbow was over 2 yards long—taller than most men. The arrows were a yard long, with flights of goose feathers (1). Arrowheads were a mixture of broad heads (2) and bodkin heads (3), which had a hardened tip capable of penetrating a man's armor at 200 paces. A trained archer could fire up to 12 arrows a minute. The best bows were cut from a yew trunk (4) with springy outer sapwood for the outside curve and compressible heartwood for the inside edge.

BATTLE LINES
On the morning of October 25, 1415, the two armies took up their positions between Agincourt and Tramecourt (1). After three hours, the English moved forward, and the mounted French knights attacked (2). They were followed by the men-at-arms, who were trampled by retreating horses and trapped by the second line of men-at-arms advancing behind them (3).
A French depiction of the battle (below right).

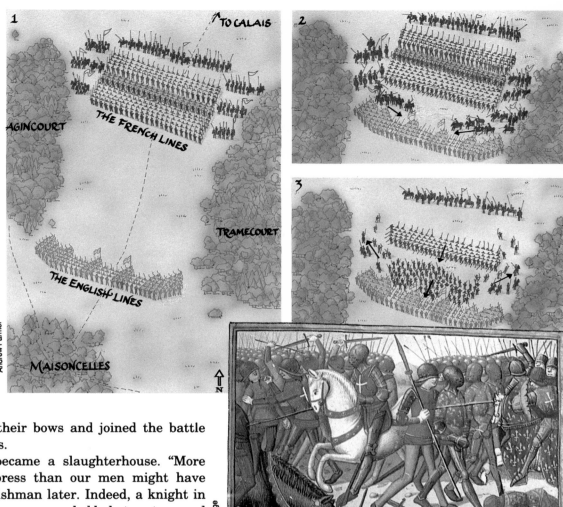

archers threw down their bows and joined the battle with swords and axes.

The battleground became a slaughterhouse. "More were dead through press than our men might have slain," wrote an Englishman later. Indeed, a knight in 50 or 60 pounds of body armor needed help to get up, and many were suffocated when others fell on top of them, as happened to Edward, Duke of York, commander of Henry's right wing. The nimble-footed archers, who "beat upon their [the French] armor with mallets as though they were smiths hammering upon anvils," enveloped the struggling French. At the same time, the French second line came on, but succeeded only in reinforcing the crush and preventing their comrades from escaping.

A TERRIBLE DEFEAT

After an hour or so, the fighting was nearly over, and the English were busy taking prisoners for ransom. Then, at about 2 p.m., the English baggage (supply train) was raided by French peasants at the same time as the French third line seemed about to attack. For a moment, the situation looked highly dangerous for the English, who were still heavily outnumbered. Henry acted at once. He ordered all but the most valuable prisoners to

THE BATTLEFIELD *(right) Agincourt today is a peaceful farming community, with little to hint at the famous battle.*

be killed to free their guards to fend off the new attack. But the throat-cutting ended when the French third line retreated. The battle of Agincourt was over.

In the three hours of battle, more than 8,500 Frenchmen were killed and France lost half its nobility—either killed or captured. The battle that was such a glorious victory for the English had cost them a mere 100-odd casualties.

At the Tournament

A knight was always ready to do battle for his king, and kept in top form by practicing his fighting skills at tournaments.

A hush falls on the assembled crowd in front of the lists. Moments later, the silence is broken by the thunderous hooves of mighty warhorses charging full tilt toward each other across the turf. The ground shakes under the weight of well over one ton of armored men and beasts as two mounted knights rush headlong into combat. Then comes a terrific crash as a lance finds its target, and a gasp from the crowd as one of the knights is hurled from his horse and sent tumbling to the ground in a tangle of limbs. Amid great cheers and shouts, the tournament has started well.

Just as we enjoy major spectacles and sporting events today, so the tournament was one of the great highlights of the medieval year. Hundreds of people attended them, from the lowest peasant to the highest lords of the land. The earliest tournaments were violent affairs, more like real battles than competitions, with many knights taking part at once. There was fighting on foot with all kinds of weapons, as well as mounted fighting. So dangerous were these tournaments that many men were

Nick Harris

killed or seriously injured, and they were eventually banned. But, in the time of Henry V, the tournament had developed into a chivalrous, ordered event, full of pomp, ceremony and color.

Tournaments were very carefully planned by special officials under the control of a "Marshal," who was licensed to arrange them by the king. They were held at specific places up and down the country, and one of the most popular sites of all was at Smithfield, near the City of London. When the time for a tournament drew near, the Marshal issued a proclamation and knights from across the land, sometimes even from countries abroad,

would enter their names to compete.

A special arena, called "the lists," was set up within the tournament grounds. The lists consisted of a long barrier, like a fence, which was the center of activity, for it was at the lists that knights jousted with each other. The ground around the lists was filled with stands of spectators; and there was a special, large stand in the middle for the king or important guests. At each end of the lists, there were enclosures for the knights to erect their tents, where they would be prepared for the contest by their squires. Behind the enclosures were grounds for exercising the warhorses. There were also

FLASH BACK

Heraldry

E T Archive

Bridgeman Art Library

Competitors' banners were inspected before a tournament to check that all the participants were honorable knights (right). Dishonorable knights were disqualified.

Heraldic emblems were a means of identifying knights in peace and war. They were reproduced on seals, stained glass (above), and surcoats (right).

Bridgeman Art Library

areas set aside for the knights who would fight on foot.

Large tournaments lasted for several days, sometimes even weeks. Before the great day arrived, knights, accompanied by their ladies, squires and servants, flocked to the tournament ground. Crowds would arrive early, hoping to gain the best viewing positions and to enjoy all the other entertainments that the tournament attracted. Musicians, jugglers, clowns, acrobats and dancing bears were as common as the tinkers and the traders who came to sell food, drink and souvenirs.

The Marshal and other officials arrived early, too, to oversee the preparations. Attempts at foul play, for example, were not uncommon; and the Marshal had to check all weapons to be used and make sure that

"arming" went according to the rules. The arming of a knight was a long and complicated process. It was carried out by his squire, usually the son of another knight who was training for knighthood. The squire had to clean and polish the armor—which was specially designed for tournaments and stronger than battle armor—and, on the great day, make sure that it was carefully laced on, piece by piece. The armor was often tailor-made for its wearer and fitted the knight like a glove, yet allowed him full movement. In most cases, a knight could climb on and off his horse, despite the great weight, with no assistance.

The tournament could not begin until the king or leading noble took up his place in the stand, for he was the lord of the tournament and the Marshal was answerable to him. And it was the lord who gave the starting signal for the first two knights to compete.

The knights rode against each other, one on each side of the lists, with their lances pointed across the barrier. Lances were blunted and always had to be aimed at the opponent's body; attempts to strike the legs often led to

A herald (below left) wore the coat of arms of his master. He helped organize tournaments, announce the combatants and keep score. But as more and more people invented coats of arms for themselves, heralds became more concerned with recording all the shields on rolls like the one shown right. Heralds were also ambassadors.

College of Arms

Keeping the score at the tournament became a complicated business, with heralds or marshals recording hits and broken lances on tally sheets like the one above.

Mansell Collection

AT PRACTICE
Young knights trained on a quintain (above), charging at the shield and then ducking to avoid the sandbag. Tournament armor was heavier and stronger than battle armor, especially the helmet (right).

Royal Armouries

disqualification, sometimes even disgrace. Each tournament, though, had its own set of rules laid down by its Marshal, covering the number of times knights could ride at each other and how many strokes with lance, sword and ax could be made. Heralds sat at the end of the lists recording the number of strokes, and their records, or tally sheets, became known as "blow-by-blow" accounts.

Sometimes, knights were knocked completely out of the saddle by the impact of a lance; sometimes the lances struck home, but shattered harmlessly. There were even times when two knights missed each other completely. Occasionally, the tournament rules allowed the knights to dismount after a number of runs along the tilt-yard and continue the contest on foot, fighting with special weapons called poleaxes, until a clear winner brought the contest to an end.

To the victor or champion went a special prize—a jewel, money, or perhaps a saddle. But the real prize for taking part and winning was the glory and honor of proving how great and skillful a knight he was. Indeed, the most successful knights won great fame with the crowds and became popular heroes, just like talented sports figures today.

FLASH BACK

Minstrels

Minstrels were professional musicians who performed at occasions like the tournament (below). Their instruments included bagpipes, the hurdy-gurdy, cornet, organetto and nakers (drums) shown left.

BPCC/Aldus Archive

Museum of London

Most nobles employed minstrels, who entertained the lords and ladies by reciting ballads and playing music. The gittern (below) was the forerunner of the modern guitar.

BBC Hutton

Ronald Sheridan

BPCC/Aldus Archive

The medieval trumpet (above) consisted of several pieces and usually measured over 2 yards long. The double trumpet (center, below) was never actually used.

Edimage

Joan of Arc

oan of Arc was one of the most remarkable women in Western history. She was born in an age when women were the virtual properties of their fathers and husbands. But Joan, an uneducated peasant woman, who would not have received the chivalrous respect given to noble ladies, was able to persuade wily politicians and hard-bitten fighting men to follow her into battle. Her enemies called her a witch; she herself and her supporters believed she was inspired by God, but she remains a puzzle. However, her achievement is a matter of history: when England seemed victorious, she inspired the French to free their land from foreign rule.

Jehanne

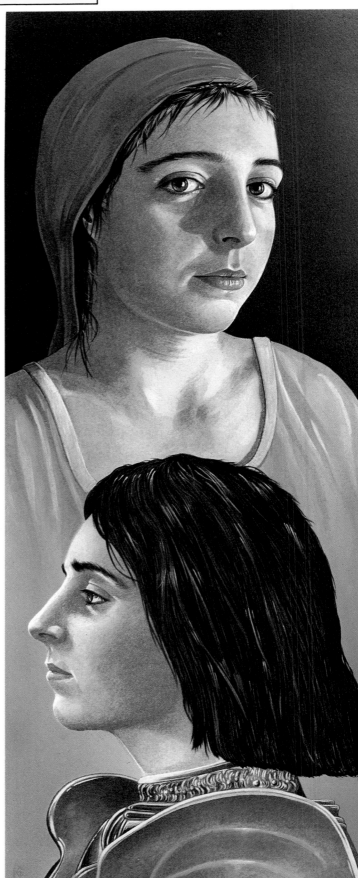

Although she was just a peasant girl, Joan of Arc was inspired by God to take up arms and fight for France.

Historians have puzzled for centuries over Joan of Arc. How did an illiterate peasant girl persuade captains, priests and princes that she would lead the French to military victory? What compelling quality gave this girl her strange power?

As a child, Joan was quiet and gentle. Her friends teased her for being "too pious," but they didn't know that she had had powerful religious experiences; for Joan had not told anyone that she had seen and heard angels. As a little girl, she was terrified to hear their ghostly voices calling to her near the village church. Soon, however, Joan began to listen and long for these voices — even though, as she grew older, their messages alarmed and confused her.

St. Michael, with St. Catherine and St. Margaret, told

TWO PORTRAITS OF JOAN as she may have looked as a 15-year-old peasant girl and an 18-year-old soldier.

Personal Profile

JOAN OF ARC *(Jehanne d'Arc)*
Born *January, 1412, in Domrémy.*
Died *May 30, 1431, when she was burned at the stake in Rouen.*
Parents *Jacques d'Arc, a well-respected farmer, and Isabelle Romée.*
Personal appearance *Short, dark-haired and stocky in build. Reasonably good-looking, but "manly" rather than pretty.*
General *Illiterate, but remarkably quick and bright. Stubborn and courageous in battle, but also compassionate and kind.*

Nik Spender

Joan that she had been chosen to save France from the English and that she must take the Dauphin, (the King of France's eldest son, normally heir to the throne), to Rheims, to be crowned Charles VII of France.

War had been raging between England and France for generations, and the peasants were heartily sick of it. The English controlled much of northern and western France, and the kings of England and France were so closely related that the war was like a family squabble. Often, the peasants didn't even know which side they were supposed to be on. Domrémy, the small village where Joan grew up, was divided by a river; on one bank, the people were allied to the English; on the side where Joan's family lived, they were loyal to the French.

GOD'S ORDERS

When the voices told Joan that she must drive the English out of her country, she wanted to believe that it was possible, but she was just a young peasant girl — she had no soldiers or weapons. Then the voices told her to go to Robert de Baudricourt, captain of the nearby town of Vaucouleurs, who would take her to the Dauphin. Joan now knew that she must leave Domrémy.

With the excuse of visiting her pregnant

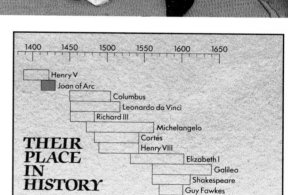

THE FAIRIES' TREE (above) Just outside Joan's village was a "magic" tree. In Lent, the children danced around it.

HOUSE IN DOMRÉMY (left) Joan lived in this stone house until she was 17. While her brothers were out in the fields, she spun indoors (above).

THEIR PLACE IN HISTORY

1400	1450	1500	1550	1600	1650

Henry V
Joan of Arc
Columbus
Leonardo da Vinci
Richard III
Michelangelo
Cortés
Henry VIII
Elizabeth I
Galileo
Shakespeare
Guy Fawkes

cousin, Joan left home, escorted by her cousin's husband, Durand Laxart. Filled with the confidence of belief in her voices, she convinced him to take her to Robert de Baudricourt instead — but Baudricourt told Laxart to box her ears and take her home. Joan, however, refused to leave, as firm in her purpose as ever. The captain then agreed to meet her, but brought his priest with him for fear that she was crazy or evil. Joan was neither, but she was extraordinarily persuasive. The two men eventually believed her story and took her to the Dauphin's court at Chinon.

The Dauphin was an unhappy, lost man. His mother, Isabelle, had disinherited him

VOICES FROM GOD

"I was 13 when I first heard a Voice from God to help and guide me. The first time I heard this Voice I was very frightened . . . When I heard it for the third time, I recognized that it was the voice of an angel."

Mary Evans

In these simple words, Joan described to the judges at her trial how she had miraculously heard the voice of St. Michael the Archangel. He spoke to her very gently: "Be a good girl and God will help you." She saw him very clearly, standing in a blaze of light, surrounded by the angels of heaven.

Soon, St. Michael was joined by two ladies wearing beautiful robes and jeweled crowns—St. Catherine and St. Margaret. They visited Joan often, coming to her in the fields or in her garden, and speaking to her in sweet and tender tones. But, eventually, they began to give her strange and terrifying orders.

They told her to liberate the city of Orléans from the English, to take the Dauphin to be crowned at Rheims and to drive the English out of France. Joan was utterly bewildered. Then, when she was 16, she was at last given clear instructions. "Go to Robert de Baudricourt, Captain of Vaucouleurs, he will give you an escort."

So Joan of Arc was launched on her inspired mission to save France.

and named her daughter's husband, Henry V of England, as the legitimate heir to the throne of France. The Duke of Burgundy, a powerful French lord, supported the English claim, and Charles had given up hope of ruling. When Joan arrived, Charles hid among his courtiers, hoping that she would go away in confusion. Instead, she picked him out easily — a miracle, since she had never before laid eyes on him — and delivered her message from God. After this meeting, the Dauphin was a changed man. Inspired by her prophecies, he believed that he was indeed the true King of France and that the English would be defeated. He gave the Maid command of his army to raise the siege of Orléans — for Joan's voices had told her she would save the stricken town.

No one has ever learned what Joan told Charles. How did she convince him of her God-given powers? Why did

he trust an ignorant peasant girl to lead his soldiers to victory? It is not surprising that many people thought Joan was a witch with magic powers.

Joan led the army into battle, yelling insults at the English and telling them to quit France in God's name. She won a decisive victory: the liberation of Orléans marked the beginning of the end of the English claims to France.

After fulfilling the first prophecy of her voices, Joan was anxious to complete her task. She escorted the Dauphin to Rheims, deep inside enemy territory. On July 17, 1429, when she was only 17 years old, she proudly took her place near the altar while her "gentil (gentle) Dauphin" was crowned King of France.

Although the prophecies were now fulfilled, Joan was impatient with Charles's refusal to consolidate the

CROWNING TRIUMPH (right) On July 17, 1429, the Dauphin was crowned King of France in Rheims Cathedral. Joan proudly watched the ceremony from the altar steps, for it was she who had driven the English out of Orléans and led the Dauphin to Rheims — just as the voices had commanded her.

Mansell Collection

THE DAUPHIN'S CORONATION COIN

A PRISONER On May 23, 1430, Joan was captured in a skirmish at Compiègne (below).

victory by taking Paris — which was then in English hands. In May, 1430, she led a small band of men against the Duke of Burgundy at Compiègne. But, when her army saw the size of the enemy force, they fled, despite Joan's urgent attempts to rally them. Far worse, she was dragged from her horse in the confusion and couldn't remount in time. Joan was now a prisoner.

She was kept in prison for a year. Once, she tried to escape by jumping from a castle tower, but was knocked out by the fall. Under constant guard, Joan was eventually taken to Rouen and put on trial. She insisted that her voices came from God, not Satan,

but the English — afraid of her power over the people — denounced her as a witch and a heretic. Joan endured three months of clever and persistent interrogation, backed by threats of torture, before she broke down and "confessed" to the charges. She was sentenced to life imprisonment on bread and water. A few days later, however, she changed her mind and courageously withdrew her confession. At once, the church court handed her over to the military to be burned as a witch.

On May 30, 1431, Joan was tied to a stake in the center of Rouen's main square, in front of a huge crowd. She cried out, calling to God and begging for a cross as the flames leapt around her. It is said that a young man in the crowd lashed two sticks together to make a cross for her to hold and that a priest fetched the golden crucifix from a nearby church and held it before the dying girl's eyes. All the onlookers — even many of the English — were moved to tears.

The cruelty of Joan's death ensured her place in history. The ordinary soldiers and peasants who had been inspired by her in life were ashamed and frightened by her execution, and one of the priests is said to have cried, "We are lost! We have burned a

tdimage

31

A MARTYR'S DEATH At the age of 19, Joan was burned at the stake in the market place of Rouen.

the trial. Twenty-five years after her death, it was officially recorded that Joan of Arc was not a witch at all, but an inspired soldier of France.

The influence of the Maid of Orléans continued for centuries after her death. The Catholic church proclaimed her a saint in 1920, and the French Resistance used her cross as their symbol of defiance during the German occupation of France in World War II. There is even a story that the invading Germans paid tribute to her as they passed through the town of Orléans, so strange and powerful has her image remained in the history of Europe.

YE WITNESS REPORTS

THE PEOPLE WHO WITNESSED JOAN'S DEATH WERE OVERCOME BY ITS CRUELTY. YEARS LATER, THEY RECALLED THEIR FEELINGS.

BROTHER LADVENU, FRIAR
"When Joan saw the fire, she told me to raise Our Lord's cross very high, so that she could see it, and this I did. While I was holding the cross before her, she begged me to get down, as the fire was rising, and I might have been burned."

WILLIAM MANCHON, COURT SCRIBE
"Afterward, I could not feel at peace. With the money I was paid for writing at the trial, I bought myself a little prayerbook, which I still have, to remind me to pray for her."

A SHOPKEEPER
"I was there on the day that Joan was burned and saw her in the flames, calling out in a loud voice, 'Jesus.' I saw many people, most of those present, weeping and bewailing for pity and saying that Joan had been unjustly condemned."

---

saint." When the flames died down, Joan's remains were gathered up and thrown into the River Seine—including her heart, which would not burn. Legends sprang up around her memory, and the peasants whispered that certain rivers now ran red because she had washed her wounds in them.

Joan's mother petitioned the King to clear her daughter's name, and eventually Charles — who had made no attempt to save her life although he owed his crown to her — set up an enquiry and commission to investigate

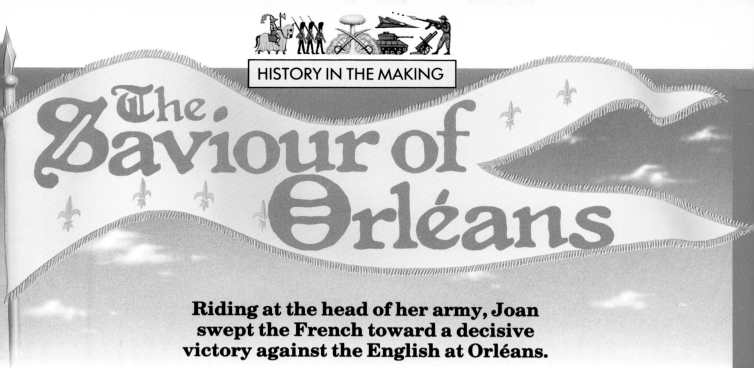

The Saviour of Orléans

Riding at the head of her army, Joan swept the French toward a decisive victory against the English at Orléans.

It was a wet and windy night when the French army approached Orléans. The English soldiers who surrounded the city had taken refuge from the weather in their forts. Within the city walls, the people waited excitedly for Joan of Arc to arrive. Rumors about the Maid, and her promise to save Orléans, had brought the citizens new hope. They had heard how, when her army was stranded on the wrong side of the river by a strong northeast wind, Joan had proclaimed that God would help them and, almost at once, the wind had changed. The army was able to sail across the river, bringing much needed supplies to the besieged city.

The next day—Friday, April 29, 1429—in darkness, rain and cold, Joan of Arc rode triumphantly through the city gates. Hundreds of people crowded the damp streets, hoping to touch the virgin sent by God to rescue them. Torches flared from their hands, from windows, on street corners; and the light glinted on her shining armor, given to her by the Dauphin himself. She was

JOAN'S MISSION
The Dauphin (left) gave Joan command of his army so that she could break the English siege of Orléans. She entered the town at nightfall on a white charger, to a rousing welcome from the townspeople.

Giraudon

33

mounted on a white charger; and at her side hung a magnificent Crusader sword which she had found hidden in the church at Fierbois, guided by her voices. Her famous banner fluttered white in the darkness—she made a splendid and inspiring sight. The citizens cheered themselves hoarse, "rejoicing as much as though they saw God himself coming among them."

Everyone knew how important it was for the French to keep control of Orléans. The city sat astride the Loire River, which divided the lands controlled by the English from the rest of France. If the English managed to take the town, they could then sweep down across the French lands to the south. The Dauphin knew that to lose Orléans was to lose France, and that Joan was his only hope of saving it.

Her own generals, however, were not convinced. They could not believe that a mad, ignorant girl understood the strategies of war. They excluded her from their

JOAN ATTACKS THE ENGLISH AT LES TOURELLES

meetings and made plans without her. In fact, she was a gifted soldier and a courageous strategist. "In God's name," she had cried, when their disobedience to her voices stranded the army on the wrong side of the river, "The Lord's counsel is better than yours . . . I bring you the help of the King of Heaven!" The ordinary soldiers, though, were inspired by her. From the day she arrived, they fought bravely to break the siege.

INTO THE FRAY

On May 4, as Joan lay resting, her voices called urgently to her "Go now to meet the English." She leaped from her bed and struggled into her armor, scolding her page: "You wicked boy, why did you let me sleep when French blood is being spilt?" Imagine her dismay as, galloping to battle, she met wounded, beaten French soldiers limping away from the field—this was not at all what she had planned.

Peter Dennis

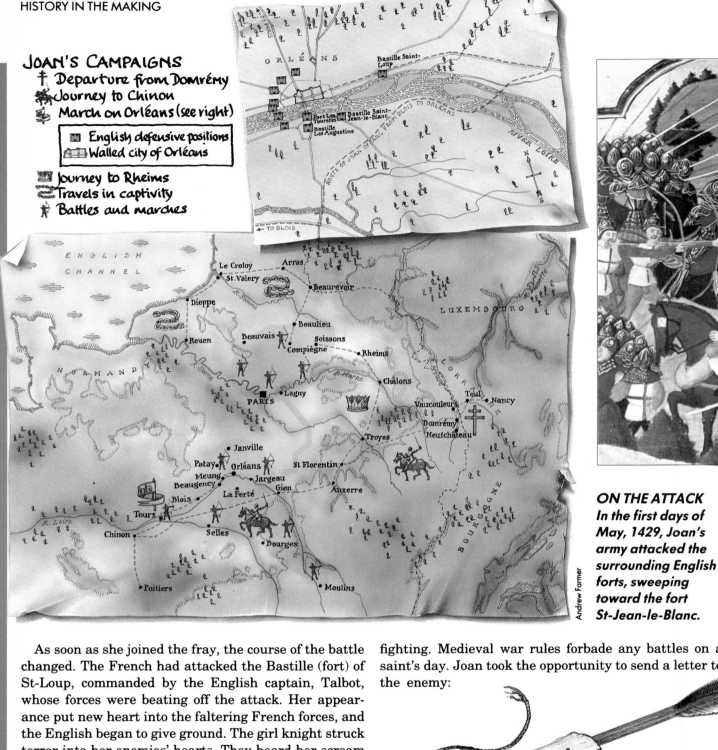

JOAN'S CAMPAIGNS
† Departure from Domrémy
✲ Journey to Chinon
⚒ March on Orléans (see right)

☐ English defensive positions
🏰 Walled city of Orléans

⚒ Journey to Rheims
✎ Travels in captivity
⚔ Battles and marches

Andrew Farmer

ON THE ATTACK
In the first days of May, 1429, Joan's army attacked the surrounding English forts, sweeping toward the fort St-Jean-le-Blanc.

As soon as she joined the fray, the course of the battle changed. The French had attacked the Bastille (fort) of St-Loup, commanded by the English captain, Talbot, whose forces were beating off the attack. Her appearance put new heart into the faltering French forces, and the English began to give ground. The girl knight struck terror into her enemies' hearts. They heard her scream over the noise of battle; they heard her soldiers roar in response. The English began to desert their leaders, filled with superstitious fear of Joan's strange powers. By nightfall, the French had overrun the Bastille, Talbot had fled, and almost all of his men were dead.

The next day, Ascension Day, there was a lull in the fighting. Medieval war rules forbade any battles on a saint's day. Joan took the opportunity to send a letter to the enemy:

You Englishmen, who have no right in the kingdom of France, the King of Heaven commands you, through me, Joan the Maid, to leave your forts and return to your own country. If not, I shall give you such a hiding that no one will ever forget it. I shall not write again.

ing—the crash of artillery bombarding the castle, the snorting of the horses and the thundering of their hooves, the yelling of the men. Suddenly, an arrow thudded into Joan's shoulder, close to her neck. She fell back, a six-inch-deep wound spouting blood "above her breast," as she had prophesied. Her soldiers began to falter, but Joan stoutly refused to give up.

Weak from loss of blood, she was helped onto her horse and advanced, yelling encouragement to the men, until the tip of her banner fluttered against the wall of the fort. She called out to the English commander: "Glasdale! Glasdale! Surrender to the King of Heaven."

Hearing these words, the terrified English fled in panic across the drawbridge, which collapsed under their weight. Glasdale and all his men fell into the river and, dragged down by their heavy armor and weapons, drowned. Weak with pain and relief and full of pity for the dead English soldiers, Joan wept as her men swept into the fortress. At long last, the battle was over.

She wrapped the letter around the shaft of an arrow and shot it into the English camp of Les Tourelles. The English responded by shouting obscene remarks at Joan.

The fighting continued for several days and, under Joan's inspired command, the French were beating down the English. By the night of Friday, May 6, all that stood between the French and victory was Glasdale's garrison, holed up in the fortress of Les Tourelles. Joan knew that victory was in sight, but she also knew that she must suffer: the night before the last battle, she warned her priest that "blood will flow from my body, above my breast."

The French captains wanted to besiege Les Tourelles rather than risk a direct attack—but Joan refused to wait. Early in the morning of May 7, she crossed the river and joined the French men-at-arms guarding the monastery of Les Augustins. Clearly outlined against the pale morning sun, she led a valiant attack on Les Tourelles from the south. The noise must have been deafen-

THE KING'S FAVOR *(above) In grateful recognition of Joan's victory, the Dauphin granted her family this special coat of arms.*

JOAN'S STATUE *This splendid monument stands in Orléans today.*

37

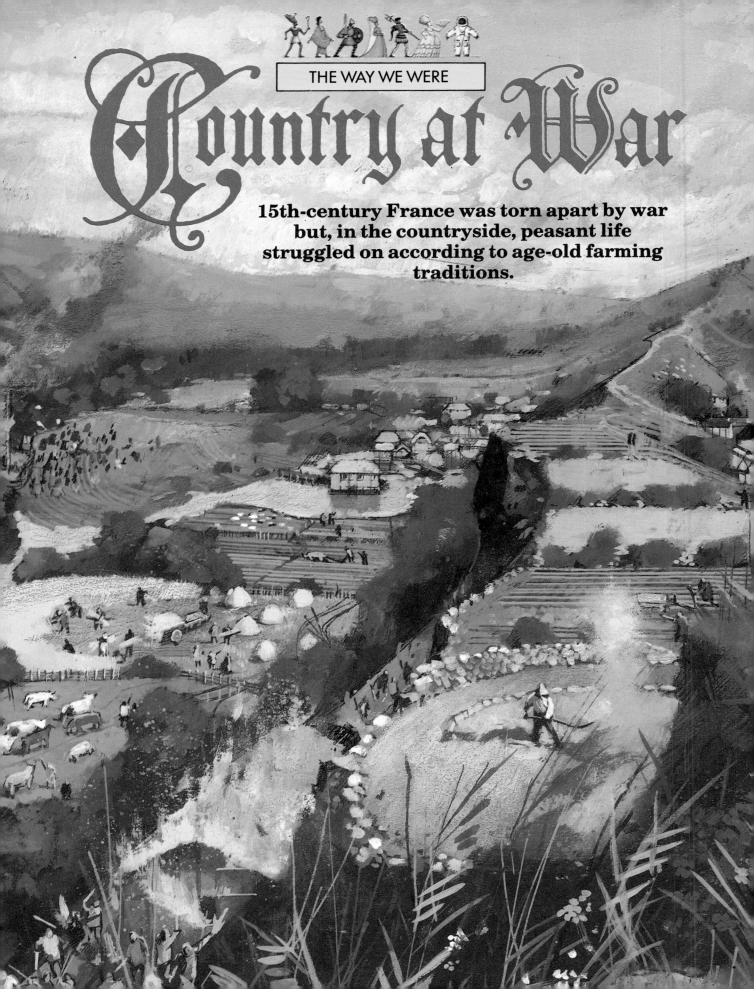

Country at War

15th-century France was torn apart by war but, in the countryside, peasant life struggled on according to age-old farming traditions.

Domrémy, Joan's birthplace, was a small insignificant village, but it was a place that symbolized the plight of France. It was divided by a river; on one side, the people belonged to Burgundy and were loyal to their English lords. On the other bank, the village was ruled by a French overlord. Soldiers from both sides were constantly skirmishing, and mercenaries traveled their rough way across the farms and pastures of the peasants.

Such was France at the turn of the 15th century. It was a land divided by opposing loyalties, torn by English and French armies, and overrun with marauding mercenaries and brigands.

This unhappy state of affairs had endured for genera-tions. Indeed, the peasants knew no other way of life. Their grandparents had lived with war raging all around them, as had their parents before them. Life in the fields and villages was guided by church bells ringing the alarm at the approach of a dangerous gang of roaming soldiers. At this somber sound, the peasants scuttled for shelter and drove their animals into secure paddocks. Wives and daughters would be hastily hidden from the rough, cruel bands of men. The alarm bell rang so often in Domrémy that the cattle would turn at its sound and take themselves off to the paddock!

Farming in the 14th and 15th centuries was also ruled by the seasons to an extent which it is hard for us to

Ivan Lapper

FLASH BACK

WORKING the LAND

Bridgeman

Philip Chidlow

Sowing seed in October (above). As the furrows are made, a sower fills them with seeds from a cloth pouch. Birds are scared away by a scarecrow dressed as an archer.

Philip Chidlow

Plowing was carried out in March, using the medieval plow which was pulled by a pair of oxen (above).

Beekeeping could be a hazardous job. To attract the swarming bees to their hives, the keepers – who wore no protective face nets – beat on iron drums to make a sound like thunder.

Earl of Leicester/Coke Estates

imagine now. The farmers had no fertilizers to help their crops increase their yield. They had no irrigation or pest control systems, and no vast nurseries to help them produce food no matter what the weather. They endured an ancient dependence on the weather conditions and life was desperately hard.

Farming followed an unchanging rhythm of working the land for food. In the winter, the fields could be cold, boggy and wet, while in summer they were dry, dusty and uncomfortably hot. The peasants plowed and weeded and hoed by hand, and prayed for the right conditions of rain and warmth, so that the wheat and barley and vegetables grew. There had to be enough to feed them through the cold dark winters.

Certain rituals had developed to mark the passage of time and give the peasants some relief from the harshness of their lives. Spring was celebrated at the start of May. Then, the peasants would lay down their plows and axes and spades. Everyone in the village decorated a special tree, or perhaps erected a symbol to spring, such as a maypole. The fresh bright weather, coming after the dreadful winter, was greeted by prayers and songs, by dancing and feasting.

Again, at the end of summer, when the peasants gathered up the crops they had tended so carefully, there were harvest festivities. Prayers were offered in gratitude, and there were often boisterous celebrations. But still the work did not stop. The men went out into the forests to find trees to chop down. They cut them into logs and dragged them back to their homes in preparation for the grim cold winter. Of course, wood or peat fires were the only source of warmth—there was no gas,

Sheep-shearing was done from late May until August (right). The farmer held the sheep firmly on its back and slowly clipped away the wool. Today, shearing is a lot faster and easier, using modern electric shears.

Bridgeman

Bridgeman

Pigs fed on acorns knocked out of trees (above left). Harvesting with a sickle (above right).

Bridgeman

Grape-picking (left) started in September. Later, the grapes were trodden for wine. Wood was cut in summer (below) and stored for winter fuel.

Mary Evans

no oil, no cozy central heating in those days. Meanwhile, the women dried, pickled or salted food in preparation for the long cold spell.

Animals played a vital part in peasant life. Every family treasured their cows, pigs, fowl and sheep. Cattle pulled plows and dragged logs or wagons. Sheep gave wool for the women to weave into cloth. And, of course, in those days you could not go to the store and buy a roast. Animals were also cherished because the peasants needed them for meat.

SOLDIERS TURNED THIEVES

But this traditional farming rhythm was disrupted in medieval France. The war had gone on for so long that the soldiers had become unruly and ill-disciplined. Often, their war lords were too poor to keep them—especially during the many periods of truce—so these men began to steal from the peasants or force them at sword-point to give up their precious supplies.

As soon as mercenaries were glimpsed across the hills, the village people went into hiding. They concealed themselves in old fortifications, or ran away to safer villages nearby. Some took refuge in moated castles or farmhouses; Joan's father used to take his family to an island in the river.

So, the peasants hid until the danger was past; but when they crept home, they were often faced with devastation. The brigands carried off the stored grain, or worse, killed the precious animals and carried off the carcasses. All their careful months of hard work could be

John Heseltine

SIGNS OF THE PAST Medieval farm buildings can still be found in the French countryside today.

destroyed in just a few hours.

It may seem amazing to us that the peasants did not try to change their lives, but their world was very narrow and physically demanding. They knew no other way of earning a living except to farm. Rural folk rarely left their villages, for roads were rough, difficult tracks—nothing like our modern highways—and carts were their only form of wheeled transport. Besides, the country roads were extremely dangerous places; travelers were often held up by brigands, and hay-wagons were ambushed and set on fire.

The vast majority of the peasant population was illiterate, so they had very little means of learning anything outside their own experience. Any news they did gather came from soldiers who occasionally camped on the edge of the village. But, for generations, such news was only of war and of who was siding with whom. The war between the French and the English went on for nearly a hundred years, and the country folk wearily accepted the disruption of their lives. This was because, for them, living in a society which was just above subsistence level there was no other life but the unceasing cycle of work on the land.

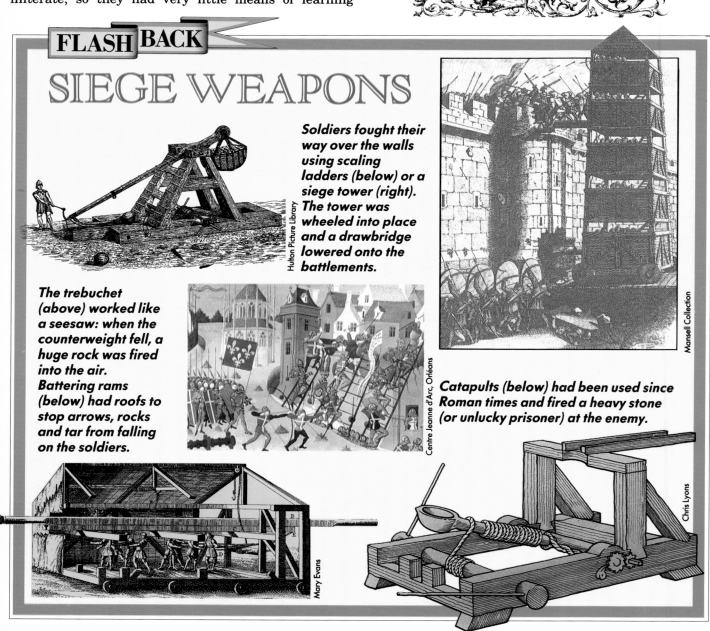

SIEGE WEAPONS

Soldiers fought their way over the walls using scaling ladders (below) or a siege tower (right). The tower was wheeled into place and a drawbridge lowered onto the battlements.

Hulton Picture Library

The trebuchet (above) worked like a seesaw: when the counterweight fell, a huge rock was fired into the air. Battering rams (below) had roofs to stop arrows, rocks and tar from falling on the soldiers.

Centre Jeanne d'Arc, Orléans

Mansell Collection

Catapults (below) had been used since Roman times and fired a heavy stone (or unlucky prisoner) at the enemy.

Mary Evans

Chris Lyons

Richard III

Until modern times, historians accepted Shakespeare's picture of Richard III as that of an evil, murderous hunchback. But the Tudors, whose own claim to the throne was weak, had an interest in blackening the name of the last Yorkist king. Today, Richard is seen as trying to provide good government for his country. However, doubts remain. He was a prime suspect in the murder of his nephews who had been placed in his care. But Richard was perhaps no worse than other nobles during the Wars of the Roses, who, as the age of chivalry came to an end, rebelled against and murdered their overlord, the king.

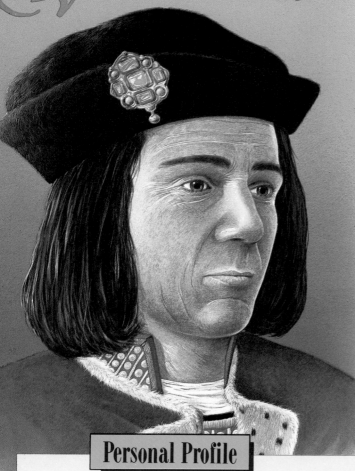

Nik Spender

Was Richard III a bloodthirsty murderer, or was his reputation unfairly blackened by history?

Skulking in the shadows, his withered arm hanging limply in a sleeve of fine silk, the evil hunchback Richard, Duke of York, plots and schemes. He wants power—the English throne—and he will stop at nothing to get it, even though many rightful heirs stand in his way. He watches with glee as his brother is executed for treason, and he remains unmoved when his little nephews are murdered. Eventually, the hunchback is crowned Richard III of England, but is killed in battle just two years later.

So ends Shakespeare's famous play, *Richard III*. For theater-goers in Shakespeare's time, this was the real lifestory of the king who had died more than 100 years earlier. Indeed, this was the portrait that passed down through history for many centuries. Only after hundreds of years did historians began to look more closely at this intriguing character to try to find out what he was really like as a king and a man.

Richard was born to the family of York in 1452, when England was on the brink of civil war. Two great rival families, York and Lancaster, were locked in a power

Personal Profile

RICHARD III
Born *October 2, 1452, Fotheringhay Castle.*
Died *August 22, 1485.*
Reign *June, 1483–August, 1485.*
Parents *Richard Plantagenet, 3rd Duke of York, and Cecily Neville.*
Marriage *Anne Neville, 1472.*
Children *Edward, 1473.*
Personal appearance *Medium height, long brown hair, small face with thin lips. Right shoulder slightly higher than the left.*
General *Brave and hardworking youth and an able general. Had nervous habit of twisting his ring.*

MIDDLEHAM CASTLE in the North Riding of Yorkshire—once a favorite home of the Earl of Warwick, and later of Richard himself. But Middleham also held sad memories for Richard. His son Edward was born here and also died here, aged 11, after a short illness. The massive 12th-century tower, the gatehouse and the chapel of Middleham still stand today (right). A detail from a window in the chapel (inset) shows Richard and his son Edward.

Geoffrey Wheeler

44

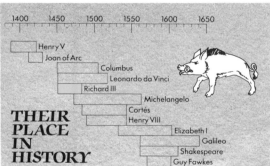

THEIR PLACE IN HISTORY

1400 1450 1500 1550 1600 1650

Henry V
Joan of Arc
Columbus
Leonardo da Vinci
Richard III
Michelangelo
Cortés
Henry VIII
Elizabeth I
Galileo
Shakespeare
Guy Fawkes

WOOING THE WIDOW

Shakespeare's Richard shamelessly courts the widow Anne at the funeral of her husband, the Lancastrian Prince Edward. Anne married Richard in 1472 and bore him a son a year later. When Anne died a year after the death of their son, it was rumored that Richard had poisoned her so that he could marry someone else.

Geoffrey Wheeler

struggle for the throne. At Richard's birth, Henry VI, a Lancastrian, ruled England, but he was a weak and feeble king. Costly wars in France had left him bankrupt, and his frequent bouts of madness left the country in turmoil.

Eventually, it was Richard's father, Richard Plantagenet, Duke of York, who attempted to remove Henry from the throne. Young Richard was just eight years old when his father seized power—though not the crown—from the Lancastrians. For Parliament decided that Henry, although he was defeated, should keep the crown until his death. Only then would it pass to the house of York. The Wars of the Roses had begun, a conflict between two important families that was to last for 30 years.

The unfortunate Duke was never to claim the crown; he and his eldest son, Edmund, were killed in battle soon after.

York's 18-year-old son, Edward, vowed revenge for his father's death, and got it only a few months later when he defeated the Lancastrians in battle. He then claimed the throne for himself and was crowned Edward

45

THE CROWN OF ENGLAND *is offered to Richard of Gloucester, at Baynard's Castle on June 26, 1483.*

IV in 1461. He rewarded his surviving brothers by making George the Duke of Clarence, and young Richard, the Duke of Gloucester.

Still only nine years old, Richard then went to live in Yorkshire, where he learned to become a gentleman and a knight. By the age of 18, he was a strong and worthy ally to his brother Edward, the king, and was true to his own motto of "Loyalty binds me." In time, Richard was entrusted with full control of the north of England,

The Cat, the Rat, and Lovell our Dog,
Rulen all England under an Hog.

A RHYME OF THE TIME *makes a play on the names of Richard's advisers, Francis, Viscount Lovell, Sir Richard Ratcliffe and Sir William Catesby.*

where he ruled fairly and gained the respect of the northerners.

But the struggle between the houses of York and Lancaster went on. With Richard's help, Edward managed to fend off a series of threats to his throne—which even included several feeble attempts by his own brother, the Duke of Clarence. Clarence was forgiven until, in 1478, he pushed his luck with Edward too far and paid with his life.

Five years later, Edward IV died, leaving the crown to his 12-year-old son, Edward. Richard was named Protector of the Realm—a caretaker king—until the young prince was old enough to rule. In the meantime, Prince Edward, and his younger brother, Prince Richard, were moved to the Tower of London to await the coronation.

Then, events took a surprising turn in favor of Richard, Duke of Gloucester. The Bishop of Bath suddenly announced that, when Edward IV had married his wife, he was already betrothed to another woman. This, he said, made the marriage invalid and meant that

RICHARD'S ARMS on a modern inn sign.

THE ROYAL FAMILY *The coronation of Richard and Anne took place at Westminster on July 6, 1483. Edward's investiture as Prince of Wales followed a month later at York.*

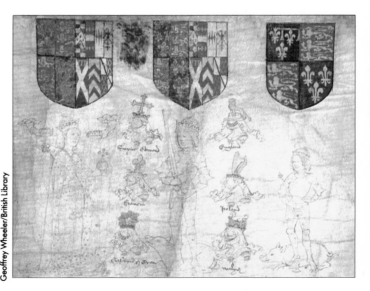

A Strange Execution

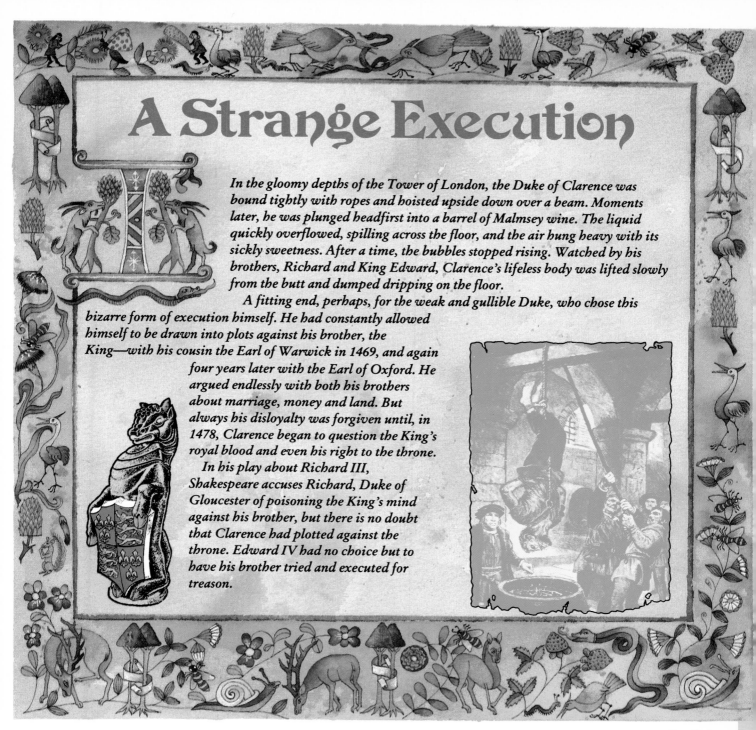

In the gloomy depths of the Tower of London, the Duke of Clarence was bound tightly with ropes and hoisted upside down over a beam. Moments later, he was plunged headfirst into a barrel of Malmsey wine. The liquid quickly overflowed, spilling across the floor, and the air hung heavy with its sickly sweetness. After a time, the bubbles stopped rising. Watched by his brothers, Richard and King Edward, Clarence's lifeless body was lifted slowly from the butt and dumped dripping on the floor.

A fitting end, perhaps, for the weak and gullible Duke, who chose this bizarre form of execution himself. He had constantly allowed himself to be drawn into plots against his brother, the King—with his cousin the Earl of Warwick in 1469, and again four years later with the Earl of Oxford. He argued endlessly with both his brothers about marriage, money and land. But always his disloyalty was forgiven until, in 1478, Clarence began to question the King's royal blood and even his right to the throne.

In his play about Richard III, Shakespeare accuses Richard, Duke of Gloucester of poisoning the King's mind against his brother, but there is no doubt that Clarence had plotted against the throne. Edward IV had no choice but to have his brother tried and executed for treason.

Susan Moxley

their sons, the two princes, had no right to the throne. Parliament then proclaimed Richard to be Edward's closest legitimate heir in June, 1483, and he was duly crowned Richard III of England on July 6.

Richard ruled wisely and well for two years, but it was a desperately difficult time.

BOAR EMBLEM A detail from the pulpit at Fotheringhay Church, Northampshire.

Geoffrey Wheeler

First, his only son died, followed only a year later by his wife. Then his crown was threatened by Henry Tudor—the last survivor of the house of Lancaster—who returned from a 14-year exile in France. Henry fought and defeated Richard at the Battle of Bosworth Field on August 22, 1485 and, with Richard's death, became Henry VII, father of Henry VIII, and grandfather of Queen Elizabeth I.

"TREASON!" Richard cried as he was hacked to death on Bosworth Field. His body was then stripped naked, slung across the back of a horse and taken to Leicester. He was buried without honors at Grey Friars, and his bones were later removed and tossed into the River Soar.

Henry even married into the York family to help strengthen his position, but he lived in fear of a rebellion by Richard's supporters. So it was that the rumors surrounding Richard's road to the throne began to grow. If Richard could be completely discredited, the threat to the new Tudors would surely fade away. Tales of Richard's terrible deeds started with claims that he had murdered the princes in the Tower. Then that he had dispatched Henry VI and his son, as well as the Duke of Clarence, and even his own wife. Before long, the rumors and accusations were written down by Tudor historians, and the myth of the monster king became accepted as fact.

WEB OF INTRIGUE

On top of all this, Richard's very appearance came under attack. He was known to have been a sickly child, and his right shoulder was a little higher than his left. No one knows for sure exactly what he looked like, but he was certainly not a hunchback. And he was an extremely able fighter in close combat, so it is unlikely that his arm was withered.

Whatever the truth, the web of intrigue surrounding the man and the myth still has to be untangled, and Richard remains the subject of much controversy to this day.

BOSWORTH FIELD as seen from Ambion Hill. It was down the northwest slope of this hill that Richard started his last valiant charge. Intent on killing Henry, Richard was overwhelmed.

MEMORIAL STONE dedicated in 1982 in Leicester Cathedral, commemorates Richard's death. Yet, if Lord Stanley and his brother William, had not held back their troops at Bosworth, Richard might have been the victor.

Personal Effects

Richard's Great Seal, (right) was used to authorize documents. The gold signet ring (bottom right) has Richard's motto engraved inside. The boar hat badge (below) was found at Bosworth.

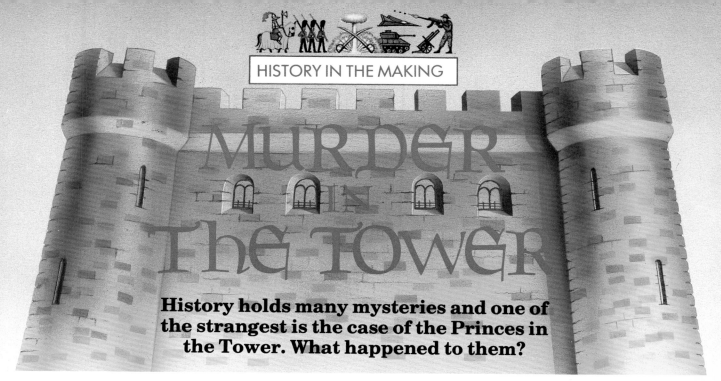

MURDER IN THE TOWER

History holds many mysteries and one of the strangest is the case of the Princes in the Tower. What happened to them?

Bridgeman/Royal Holloway and Bedford New College

In 1483, Prince Edward succeeded to the throne when his father, Edward IV, died of a fever on April 9. The 12-year-old boy moved into spacious royal apartments in the Tower of London, then a palace, as well as a prison, on May 5, and was later joined there by his younger brother, Richard of York. The boys spent their days playing and preparing for Edward's coronation. Then on June 22, it was announced that Edward had been declared illegitimate; and his uncle, Richard of Gloucester, was to be made king instead.

The bewildered boys suddenly found that their home had become their prison and except for a few servants, they had no further contact with the outside world. For a few weeks, they could be seen playing in the grounds; then they were seen only at the windows of the Tower. By August, they had vanished from view completely.

The disappearance of the two young princes has remained a mystery for more than five centuries. Some people believe that the boys were murdered, right there in the Tower; others say that they were simply

THE TWO PRINCES are believed to have been murdered by Richard III (right, top). But Henry Stafford, Duke of Buckingham (center) and Henry VII (bottom) also had the motive and the opportunity.

Fotomas   Geoffrey Wheeler   National Portrait Gallery

spirited out of the country, where they would no longer be a threat to the English Crown.

But if the boys were murdered, who could have committed such an evil crime? Who stood to gain most from their deaths? It is interesting to examine the main suspects and their motives.

RICHARD III—GUILTY OR NOT?

According to Tudor historians, Richard decided that the princes should die and charged Sir James Tyrell—whom he knew to be an ambitious man—to carry out the deed. Sir James, keen to gain the King's favor, found two assassins for the job: Miles Forest, one of the men in charge of the boys, and John Dighton, Sir James's own horsekeeper.

On the fateful evening, Forest and Dighton crept into the Tower. As the princes slept, the assassins sneaked through the door into their bedroom. They each took a feather pillow and quickly pushed it down over the faces of the sleeping boys.

Edward and Richard woke at once and tried to

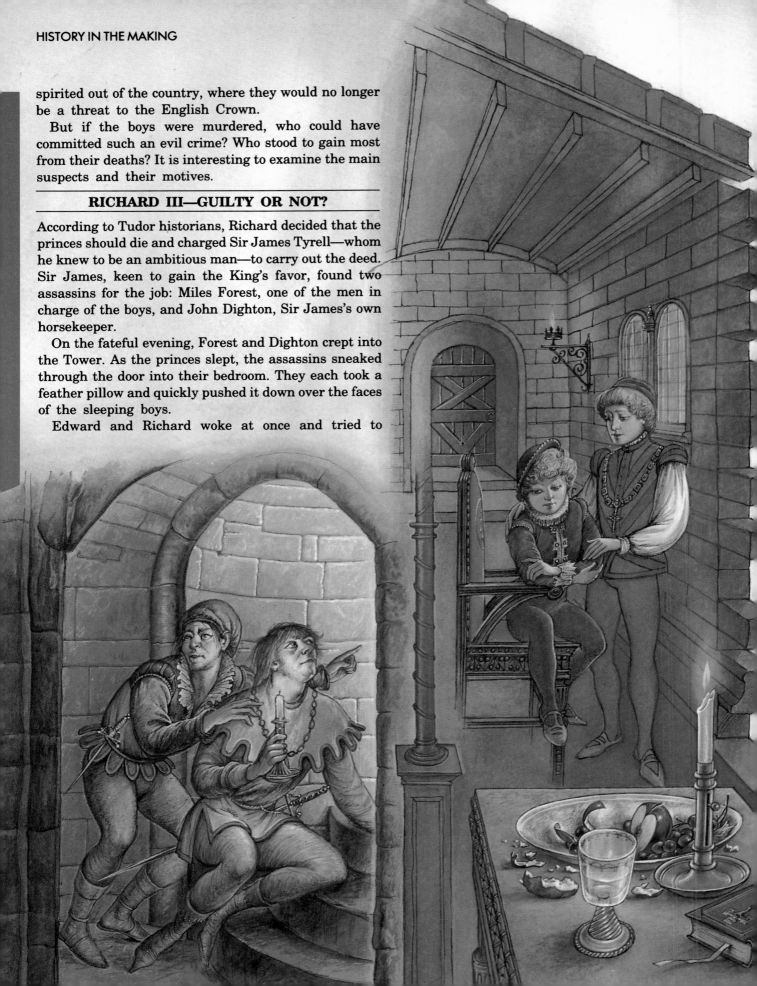

struggle free. But they were no match for the fully grown men. The pillows muffled their pathetic cries for help, and soon they stopped struggling. The men quickly removed the bodies and buried them at the foot of some stairs, under a pile of stones.

So runs the Tudor case against Richard. But it can be strongly argued that Richard had no pressing reason to kill the boys—he already had the Crown and had been accepted by the people. The princes were harmless to him as long as they were imprisoned or kept under guard in exile. On the other hand, if the boys were alive, why did he not produce them and clear his name? And

George Thompson

SCENE OF THE CRIME
The battlements (A) where the princes played before they were supposedly murdered in the "Bloody Tower" (B).

IN SANCTUARY
Queen Elizabeth reluctantly allows her son Richard to leave the sanctuary of Westminster with the Archbishop of Canterbury (left). The boy joined his brother Edward in the Tower of London to help prepare for his coronation.

ROYAL PHYSICIAN
Dr John Argentine (below) was one of the last people to see the princes alive when he attended Edward at the Tower of London (right). In 1501, Argentine was made Provost of King's College, Cambridge.

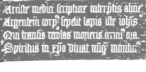

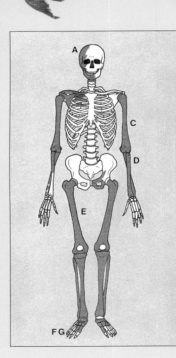

Royal

Edward II

The shaded areas show those bones buried in Westminster Abbey in 1933. The humeri (C), ulnae (D), femora (E), and fifth metatarsal bones (F) are

there is no evidence which shows that Richard was *not* involved.

HENRY VII—GUILTY OR NOT?

Henry Tudor claimed the throne after the death of Richard III on the shakiest of grounds. His great-grandmother was the illegitimate daughter of John of Gaunt, third surviving son of Edward III. Assuming that the two boys were still alive—and at this time, there was no evidence to suggest they were not—they would have posed a serious threat to Henry. As the last male survivors of the house of York, their claim to the throne was stronger than his own.

Also, Henry had married Elizabeth, the boys' sister, and had her declared legitimate. This in effect also legitimized her brothers, making them even more of a threat to

Henry's position. In this sense, Henry had far more to gain from the boys' deaths than Richard.

BUCKINGHAM—GUILTY OR NOT?

Another suspect was Henry Stafford, Duke of Buckingham. Once a loyal supporter of Richard, he joined forces with the Tudors and led a rebellion against Richard three months after his coronation. But his motives could be suspect. Instead of switching loyalty to Henry Tudor, he may have had designs on the throne himself, through his lineage

MISSING BONES
It was in 1674, in the reign of Charles II (right), that two skeletons were found in the Tower. Because they were assumed to be the remains of the Yorkist princes, they were set aside for reburial. But four years elapsed before they were interred, and in that time, some of the bones were stolen and replaced with animal bones.

Public Records Office

with Thomas Woodstock, the youngest of Edward III's children.

As Constable of England, Buckingham had access to the boys in the Tower. But guilty or not, he did not live to reap any benefits. Richard learned of his treachery and had him beheaded.

EXHIBIT A—THE BONES

So we have three suspects, each with similar motives. But what about hard evidence? No bodies were found during the lifetime of Richard or of Henry. It was not until two centuries later that workmen digging, near the White Tower in 1674, found a chest buried in the foundations of a staircase. Inside were the skeletons of two children. It was assumed they were the remains of the two young princes, and the bones were later placed in Westminster Abbey.

In 1933, the bones were removed from the Abbey for further study. Examination revealed that the bones came from children, aged 10 and 12, of the same family. But the tests could not establish whether the children were male or female, nor could they pinpoint the actual date of death.

So, without conclusive evidence, the truth remains a mystery. What do you think happened to the princes in the Tower?

ROOM FOR DOUBT?
It is said that this white marble urn in Westminster Abbey (below) holds the bones of the princes. But unless tests can be made that could prove both the sex and the date of death, there is still doubt as to their identity.

Geoffrey Wheeler

shown together for comparison. The first metatarsals (G) and skull (A) are from "Edward's" skeleton, part of the skull (B) from "Richard's."

THE WAY WE WERE

Families at War

In the 30 years between 1455 and 1485, England was torn apart as the families of York and Lancaster fought for the throne.

In their cottage at Wakefield, in the north of England, John and Daniel Chater look as close as any brothers could hope to be. Yet only three years before, in 1485, they were fighting on opposite sides in a bloody war. Happy to be united again, they begin to look back over the long years of conflict that had split the family.

"It really started way back when we were lads, over half a century ago," John began. "Henry VI took the throne as soon as he was 16, but he wasn't really up to the job. He was a simple man—quite mad

Susan Moxley

A QUARREL in the Temple Gardens, London, led the Lancastrians and the Yorkists to pick their red and white "rose" emblems.

Bridgeman

like his grandfather, they say, and easily influenced by others at court, especially his French wife, Margaret of Anjou. The long years of war with France had cost him a fortune, and his debts and fumbling mismanagement of the country eventually led to rebellion in 1450. Then Richard Plantagenet, Duke of York, who had more royal blood in his veins than the king, thought he could do a better job . . .!"

"Yes," Daniel broke in, "Richard wanted to be king, and in 1452 he decided to take the throne by force. He couldn't get enough support, though, and retreated to one of his Welsh castles. But he got his chance a year later, when the king went soft in the head and Richard was named Protector."

"And to think that was when you and I came to blows," John continued, "just because we were working for the richest and most powerful families in these parts. I worked for Richard's allies, the Nevilles, remember? And you were a stable lad for the Percys, who supported the King and the house of Lancaster."

"We first found ourselves fighting in May, 1455," Daniel butted in. "As Protector, Richard had been at loggerheads with Queen Margaret until Henry got his senses back at Christmas. Then Richard lost his position of power and doubled his efforts to seize the Crown. Things came to a head in May, and you and me found ourselves on opposite sides of a double row of archers,

BATTLEGROUNDS The map shows the main battles between the Houses of York and Lancaster, and some of their strongholds.

MORTIMER

PERCY

NEVILLE

RICHARD III

CLIFFORD

WARWICK

YORK

Battle of
Redgeley Moor 1464
DUNSTANBURGH
ALNWICK
WARKWORTH
WARK
NEWCASTLE
Battle of
Hexham 1464
BYWELL
CARLISLE

BARNARD
BOLTON
RICHMOND
SHERIFF
HUTTON
YORK
Battle of Towton 1461
Fought in the snow
PONTEFRACT

DENBIGH
CHESTER
RUTHIN
HARLECH

Battle of Wakefield 1460
Richard Duke of York killed

NEWARK
BELVOIR
TATTERSHALL
CAISTER

Battle of
Blore Heath 1459
Battle of
Bosworth 1485
Battle of Lose-Coat Field
1470
Coats left on field

Duke of Somerset
executed 1471
LUDLOW
Battle of
Ludford 1459
KENILWORTH
WARWICK
Battle of
Northampton 1460
FOTHERINGHAY
FARMING
IPSWICH
Tower of
London

Battle of Tewkesbury
1471
Battle of
Edgecote 1469

MILFORD HAVEN
PEMBROKE

GLOUCESTER
BERKELEY
CARDIFF

Battles of St Albans
1455   1461
Battle of Barnet 1471
Earl of Warwick killed
LONDON
SANDWICH
Jack Cade
rebellion
1450
DOVER
HYTHE
ROMNEY
WINCHELSEA
HASTINGS
HURSTMONCEUX

..ury Tudor arrives
..lford Haven
.. August 1485
GOLDSMITHS
QUARRYING
BUILDING
MATERIALS

PLYMOUTH

Ship building at "Cinque Ports"

BEAUCHAMP

BEAUFORT

RICHARD III

Lancastrian victories
Yorkist victories
Lancastrian castles
Yorkist castles

N
S

Andrew Farmer

FLASH BACK

Family Strongholds

Image Bank

Mansell

Alnwick Castle in Northumberland (left) belonged to the rich and powerful Percy family.

Headquarters for Richard III's government in Wales, Ludlow Castle (right) was a Yorkist stronghold. It was here that Prince Edward heard of his father Edward IV's death.

Airviews

The Lancastrians at Harlech Castle in North Wales (above) came under siege by the Yorkist Lord Herbert in 1464. They held out until the summer of 1468, then surrendered to Lord Herbert.

Geoffrey Wheeler

The ruins of Barnard Castle, County Durham (above). This Beauchamp stronghold fell to Richard III, along with Warwick Castle (right) and other properties, through his marriage to Anne (Beauchamp) Neville. Richard used Pontefract Castle (above right) as his headquarters when he became Constable of England in 1472.

Mansell

On the coast of Northumbria, Bamburgh Castle (right) was lost by the Percy family in 1464. It reverted to Sir Ralph after he swore allegiance to Edward IV.

John Bethell

just outside St Albans in Hertfordshire."

"That's right," continued his brother, "You wore the red rose of Lancaster, and I the white rose of York. It wasn't much of a fight though, was it? Barely two hours passed before we took control of the King, who had three arrow wounds in his face. Richard was made Protector again, and we had about four years of peace, but the people suffered great hardship. Then you fought on the King's side in two battles in '59. The decisive one was at Ludford Bridge in October. The King promised Yorkist soldiers a pardon if they surrendered, and it turned into a rout."

"The tables were turned at Northampton, though," Daniel remarked. "It was a disaster. We fought for only half an hour. The commander of the royal vanguard deserted to the Yorkists, and they captured the king."

John took up the story. "Then Richard persuaded parliament to make him king on Henry's death. But, at the start of winter, he made the mistake of coming north to Wakefield. The Queen had secretly gathered an army of 150,000 men and launched a surprise attack on York at Wakefield. Greatly outnumbered, York and his son Edmund were killed in battle the day before New Year's Eve."

"His son Edward was quick to take revenge, though," interrupted Daniel. "By February, he had beaten us at Mortimer's Cross and marched to London to claim the crown. In the meantime, though, the queen's troops marched on to St Albans. The Earl of Warwick tried to stop us there, but his line of attack quickly crumbled and he fled to join forces with Edward. Although the Queen was reunited with Henry, she let victory slip through her fingers."

"Yes," said John, "Edward and Warwick marched into London on February 26, 1461, to a jubilant welcome. Edward was proclaimed King at the beginning of March, and by the end of the month, we'd fought one of the biggest and bloodiest battles of the wars. All told, 28,000 men lost their lives when we thrashed the Lancastrians at Towton, in a snowstorm. The Queen and Henry ran off to seek refuge in Scotland.

"We had two more victories in 1464—at Hedgeley Moor and Hexham—and, for five years, the Crown seemed safe in Yorkist hands. Looking back like this shows how little fighting we really did during those 30 years of war. Only about 61 weeks in all!"

But John was getting side-tracked, and Daniel was impatient to continue. "There was more discontent in 1469, and at one point, Warwick—they called him 'the Kingmaker'—joined with Edward's brother, Clarence, to seize the throne. They marched north, and clashed with loyal Yorkists near Banbury in the summer. Soon, Warwick had captured Edward, and tried for a while to rule the country himself. But he didn't have enough support to stop the rioting, and Edward took control again."

Geoffrey Wheeler

Geoffrey Wheeler

AT TEWKESBURY on May 4, 1471, the Yorkists gained a decisive victory (top). Two days after the battle, the Duke of Somerset was beheaded (above). For Queen Margaret (left), it was the final disaster. Her son, Edward, was killed in battle, she was captured and imprisoned in the Tower of London, and her husband, Henry VI, died, probably murdered.

FLASH BACK

Royal Armouries

WEAPONS OF WAR

Battles were fought mainly on foot, using close hand-to-hand weapons. Hand weapons included various types of sword (A, B), daggers (C, D), war hammers (E), pole-axes (F), and different forms of the mace (G).

A

B

C

D

Men-at-arms used their hand weapons to crush the enemies armor. The weight of armor meant that battles were exhausting. Few lasted more than a few hours.

Spearmen and billmen used their long-handled weapons to cut and thrust. The hook shape of the bill (above) was used to unseat riders.

E

F

G

A shaft from a crossbow (left) could pierce through armor at up to 50 yards. However, a longbow could fire up to 10 arrows to the crossbow's two!

Richard Hook

"Yes," continued John, "and Edward learned a lesson in treachery. In March, 1470, we put down another rebellion by Clarence and Warwick near Stamford. Taken by surprise, their men were in such a hurry to escape, they left their coats where they lay in the fields—one contained evidence of Clarence's treachery. We called it the 'Battle of Lose-coat Field!' After that, Clarence and Warwick ran off to France!"

"But they returned in October and put Henry back on the throne," interrupted Daniel. "Edward himself had to flee then."

"He wasn't gone long, though, was he?" sneered John. "Five months later, he'd brought a fleet of ships back to Humberside, and by April, Londoners were waving

white roses again. We beat the Lancastrians at Barnet in April on Easter Sunday, killing that traitor Warwick, and at Tewkesbury in May, when Henry's son, Edward was killed. Those two battles sealed the fortunes of the house of York; and, when Edward had done away with Clarence and the old King, there were no real threats to the throne. Then Edward died in 1483, and his brother Richard took over . . ."

"Then Henry Tudor landed in England in '85," Daniel butted in, "and killed Richard in the battle of Bosworth Field in August 1485. And it looks like the Tudors are here to stay, eh, John?" His brother nodded.

GLOSSARY

baggage Everything an army needs on maneuvers, including tents, clothing, and provisions.

bastille (French) A tower for the defense of a fortress, or any fortified building.

betrothed Promised in marriage, or engaged to be married.

bill A military weapon used by English infantry in the 13th and 14th centuries.

billman An **infantry** soldier who was armed with a bill.

brigand A robber or bandit who lives by plundering others.

charger A powerful horse that a soldier rides into battle.

chivalrous The way a knight ought to behave: brave, courteous, noble, and always there to protect the weak and poor.

chronicler One who writes about the events of the time, recording them in the order that they happened.

coat of arms A knight's own design, embroidered on a **surcoat** and worn over his armor, so that he might be recognized in battle.

Constable The highest ranking officer in the royal court, in charge of the army and responsible for keeping peace.

cornet A woodwind instrument of medieval times, similar in appearance to an oboe.

counterweight A weight equal to another, but working as an opposite force to it.

crusade Military expedition to the Holy Land, which had the blessing of the Church.

Dauphin (French) The title given to the eldest son of the French king, dating from 1350 and last used in 1830.

dub To make someone a knight, done by tapping him on the shoulders with a sword.

effigy Any likeness or image of a person, such as a statue, or head stamped on a coin.

falconry An ancient sport or pastime that involves the training of falcons or hawks to hunt small game.

fertilizer Substances, such as manure or chemicals, that are added to the soil to feed and nourish plants, and encourage strong growth.

feudalism Social order in the Middle Ages in which nobles held land in exchange for service to their overlord.

gittern A musical instrument that looked like an ornate violin, but was in fact a very early guitar. It had four strings and was played with a plectrum.

herald An official messenger who went to the enemy under safe conduct to declare war, or peace, on behalf of his leader.

hurdy-gurdy A stringed musical instrument shaped like a small piano with a handle. When the handle is cranked, it makes a wheel pass across the strings, and the music plays.

infantry Soldiers who fight on foot.

interrogation Asking questions in a demanding manner, to make a person tell everything he or she knows.

intriguing Fascinating and puzzling, full of exciting mystery.

invalid Not recognized by law and therefore has not officially happened, or taken place.

investiture The ceremony held when land and all that belongs to it, is officially given to another.

irrigation Supplying land with water, by building canals, ditches, or waterways, so that plants may grow.

joust To fight on horseback, with a lance, against another competitor in a tournament. Also called tilting.

liberate To set free.

lineage Parents and relatives, and their parents and relatives, and so on, back through history. The family tree.

lists Two lanes, divided by a rail, down which two knights would **joust**—charge at one another on horseback. Also the area enclosed to hold a jousting tournament.

mace A long-handled club, often with metal and spikes at one end. It was used in the wars of the Middle Ages to break armor.

martyr Someone who has beliefs so strong that he or she is prepared to die for them.

mercenary A soldier who is willing to fight for a foreign army, for pay.

naker A small kettledrum, played with wooden sticks. Usually two, each with a different sound, were played together.

pitched battle A battle that has been planned before the fight starts, so that each group of soldiers knows in advance exactly where it is attacking.

poleax A long-handled ax, used in battle.

Prince of Wales A title given to the eldest son of the king or queen of England. It was first used in this way in 1301.

quintain A target that hung from a cross-bar attached to a post, that was used in tilting (see **joust**).

ransom The price that has to be paid for the release of someone who has been captured or taken prisoner.

Resistance Secret organizations formed in World War II, to fight the Nazi Germans when they occupied other European countries. They included civilians and guerilla fighters, who were helped by the Americans and British.

Riding A third part of a county in England, such as Yorkshire, which was made up of North Riding, East Riding and West Riding.

rollicker Someone who likes to have great fun, and does so in a noisy, careless, and lively way.

rout A disorderly fight.

scribe A person employed to copy books by hand before printing was invented. Also used by kings to write letters, court information, and manuscripts.

skirmish A short fight between small groups of fighters; part of a major battle.

squire The son of a noble, who, from an early age, worked as a servant to a knight in order to train to be a knight himself.

surcoat A simple coat, or sleeveless tunic, worn over clothes or armor. The owner's "arms" were embroidered on a surcoat worn over armor, providing the origin of the term **coat of arms**.

tally sheet The piece of paper used to keep scores or records of competitive events, which can then be counted, or tallied, to find the best score.

terrain A piece of land, but in relation to its fitness for a purpose.

tilt-yard Where jousting and tilting took place.

trebuchet (French) A medieval war machine that hurled large rocks. It used a **counterweight,** which was held high, suspended on the end of a pole that was balanced on a support. When the weight was allowed to drop, it hurled a slightly lighter weight that was held at the other end of the pole, through the air.

troubadour A musician-poet of the 11th to 13th centuries. He composed songs and poems on the themes of chivalry and love.

CHRONOLOGY

The End of Chivalry 1300–1500

	POLITICS AND WAR	SCIENCE AND DISCOVERY
1300 to 1350	**1301** Wales becomes the principality of the heir to the English throne. **1306** Robert Bruce is crowned King of Scotland. He is defeated by the English in two battles. **1314** Battle of Bannockburn. Robert Bruce defeats the English and wins independence for Scotland. **1317** Salic Law in France bans women from inheriting the crown. **1337** Hundred Years' War between France and England begins. **1340** Battle of Sluys. English under Edward III defeat French. **1346** Battle of Crécy. English defeat French.	**1303** First medical reference to eyeglasses. **1305** Edward I of England standardizes the yard and the acre. **c.1320–1324** Italian philosopher, Marsilius of Padua, writes *Defender of the Peace,* which attacks the power of the Church. **1324** Marco Polo, traveler to China, dies. **1349** William of Ockham, founder of Nominalist philosophy, dies. **c.1350** Firearms first used in Europe.
1351 to 1400	**1356** Battle of Poitiers. English defeat the French and capture their king, John II. **1360** Treaties of Brétigny and Calais. War ends between England and France until 1369. English given large areas of France. **1372** French capture Poitou and Brittany from the English. **1399** Henry Bolingbroke deposes English king, Richard II, and becomes Henry IV.	**1358** Jean Buridan, French philosopher of science, dies. **1363** Guy de Chauliac writes *Chirurgia Magna,* a textbook of surgery. **c.1370** The steel crossbow first used as a weapon in warfare. **1382** Nicholas Oresme, pioneering economist, scientist, and advisor to the French king, dies.
1401 to 1450	**1400–1415** Rebellion in Wales against English rule, by Owen Glendower. **1406** James I becomes King of Scotland. He is captured by English and imprisoned. **1415** Battles of Agincourt and Harfleur. English, under Henry V, defeat the French. **1420** Treaty of Troyes. Henry V made heir to the French king. **1422** Henry V dies. Succeeded by weak son, Henry VI. **1429** Town of Orléans saved from English siege by Joan of Arc. **1431** Joan burned as a witch in Rouen. **1436** French capture Paris. **1449** French capture Normandy.	**1405** Konrad Kyeser writes *Bellifortis,* a book on the technology of war. **c.1427** Portuguese sailors reach the Azores. **1437** Prince Henry the Navigator founds the Portuguese colonial institute. **c.1440** Nicholas of Cusa, theologian, scientist, mathematician, and philosopher, writes *On Learned Ignorance.* **c.1440** Johann Gutenberg invents printing using movable type.
1451 to 1500	**1453** Hundred Years' War ends, with England keeping only the town of Calais. **1455** Wars of the Roses begin in England. **1461** Battle of Mortimer's Cross. Henry VI defeated. Succeeded by Edward IV. **1470** Battle of Edgecote. Edward IV defeated and flees abroad. Henry VI regains crown. **1471** Battle of Barnet. Henry VI defeated and killed. Edward IV regains crown. **1483** Edward IV dies. Succeeded by son, Edward V, but he is killed, probably by Richard III. **1485** Battle of Bosworth Field. Richard III defeated by Henry Tudor, who becomes Henry VII and founds Tudor dynasty.	**1470** First French printing press set up at the Sorbonne, Paris. **1473** Copernicus, Polish astronomer, born. **1476** William Caxton sets up first English printing press at Westminster. **1487-1488** Bartholemew Diaz sails around Cape of Good Hope, South Africa. **1492** Christopher Columbus reaches West Indies on his first voyage. **1497** John Cabot discovers Newfoundland.

The knight's profession was war, and as the age of chivalry came to an end between the years 1300 and 1500, there was plenty of fighting to occupy him. During the Hundred Years' War, the English and French fought for the throne of France, while, in the Wars of the Roses, unruly English nobles battled for control of their kingdom.

RELIGION AND SOCIETY	ART AND LITERATURE	
1302 Pope Boniface VIII proclaims his superiority over secular kings and other rulers. 1303 Philip IV of France imprisons the Pope, who dies soon after. 1305 A Frenchman is elected Pope Clement V. 1307–1314 The Knights Templar, a religious order, are investigated for heresy. 1309 Papacy moves to Avignon, France. 1347–1351 Black Death (bubonic plague) kills about one-third of European population.	c.1300 Guillaume de Machaut, French composer, born. 1304 Italian poet, Petrarch, born. c.1305 Giotto, one of the founders of modern painting, paints frescoes for the Arena Chapel, Padua. 1311–1321 Dante Aligheri, one of the greatest Italian poets, writes *The Divine Comedy*. c.1318 Duccio de Buoninsegna, first great Sienese painter, dies.	**1300 to 1350**
1358 Jacquerie (peasant uprising) defeated by French nobles. c.1378 English scholar, John Wycliffe, calls for the reform of the Church. 1378 Pope Urban VI returns Papacy to Rome. 1378 Rival French Pope, Clement VII, elected at Avignon. "Great Schism" begins. 1380 First translation of the Bible into English by Wycliffe. 1381 Led by Wat Tyler, the English peasants revolt against the impositon of a poll tax. The revolt is crushed by the Government.	c.1353 Boccaccio completes his collection of tales, *The Decameron*. c.1370 William Langland writes English poem, *Piers Plowman*. 1385 John Dunstable, English composer, born. c.1386 Donatello, first great Florentine sculptor, born. 1387 Geoffrey Chaucer writes *The Canterbury Tales*.	**1351 to 1400**
1409 Council of Pisa called. The two rival Popes are deposed, and a new Pope is elected. The two Popes refuse to stand down. 1414-1418 Council of Constance. All three existing Popes are deposed. Martin V is elected the one true Pope and rules from Rome. 1417 "Great Schism" ends.	c.1401 French poet, Jean Froissart, completes his chronicles of the Hundred Years' War. 1408–1409 Donatello carves statue of *David*. 1413–1416 Limbourg brothers illustrate *Les Très Riches Heures* (The Very Rich Hours) for the Duke of Berry in France. 1420 Brunelleschi designs dome of Florence Cathedral. 1431–1438 John Lydgate writes English poem, *The Fall of Princes*. 1434 Jan van Eyck paints *The Arnolfini Wedding*.	**1401 to 1450**
1471 Thomas à Kempis, author of influential theological work, *Imitation of Christ*, dies. 1483 Martin Luther born. 1484 Pope condemns the practice of witchcraft. Inquisitors sent to Germany to try witches. 1494 Treaty of Tordesillas. Pope divides Americas between Spain and Portugal—ignored by other European countries.	1452 Leonardo da Vinci born. c.1460 Giovanni Bellini paints *The Agony in the Garden*. 1461 French poet, François Villon, writes his *Testament*. 1485 William Caxton prints the *Morte D'arthur*, a collection of stories about King Arthur by Sir Thomas Malory. 1475 Michelangleo born. 1489 John Skelton appointed court poet to Henry VII of England.	**1451 to 1500**

FURTHER READING

Barnie, John, *War in Medieval English Society: Social Values in the Hundred Years' War, 1337-1399*. Cornell University Press (Ithaca, 1974)

De Angeli, Marguerite, *The Door in the Wall*. Scholastic Inc. (New York, 1984)

Earle, Peter, *The Life and Times of Henry V*. Biblio Distribution Center for Weidenfeld & Nicolson (Totowa, 1972)

Fisher, Leonard E., *The Tower of London*. Macmillan (New York, 1987)

Garry-McCord, Kathleen, *Dick Whittington*. Troll Associates (Mahwah, 1981)

Gies, Frances, *Joan of Arc: The Legend and the Reality*. Harper & Row (New York, 1981)

Lasker, Joe, *Tournament of Knights*, Harper & Row Junior Books (New York, 1986)

Lucie-Smith, Edward, *Joan of Arc*. Norton (New York, 1977)

Manning, Rosemary, *Heraldry*. Dufour Editions (Chester Springs, 1966)

Morris, Neil and Ting, *The Queen of the Tournament*. Silver, Burdett & Ginn (Lexington, 1986)

Nichol, Jon, *Battle of Agincourt*. Longman (White Plains, 1974)

Ross, Charles, *Richard III*. University of California Press (Berkeley, 1982)

Rutland, Jonathan, *Knights and Castles*. Random House (New York, 1987)

Saunders, Susan, *The Tower of London*. Bantam Books (New York, 1984)

Seward, Desmond, *Richard III: England's Black Legend*. Watts, Franklin (Danbury, 1984)

Seward, Desmond, *The Hundred Years' War: The English in France, 1337-1453*. Atheneum (New York, 1978)

Shakespeare, William, *Henry V*. Oxford University Press (New York, 1982)

Stevenson, Robert Louis, *Black Arrow*. Airmont (New York, 1964)

Storr, Catherine, *Joan of Arc*. Raintree Publications (Milwaukee, 1985)

Wilkinson, Frederick, *Arms and Armor*. Watts, Franklin (New York, 1984)

Windrow, Martin, *The Medieval Knight*. Watts, Franklin (New York, 1986)

INDEX